Domesticated Glory

Domesticated Glory
How the Politics of America Has Tamed God

GALE HEIDE

◆PICKWICK *Publications* • Eugene, Oregon

DOMESTICATED GLORY
How the Politics of America Has Tamed God

Copyright © 2010 Gale Heide. All rights reserved. Except for brief quotations in critical publications or reviews, no part of this book may be reproduced in any manner without prior written permission from the publisher. Write: Permissions, Wipf and Stock Publishers, 199 W. 8th Ave., Suite 3, Eugene, OR 97401.

Scripture quotations marked (NASB) are from the NEW AMERICAN STANDARD BIBLE®. Copyright © 1960, 1962, 1963, 1968, 1971, 1972, 1973, 1975, 1977, 1995 by The Lockman Foundation. Used by permission. All rights reserved.

Pickwick Publications
An Imprint of Wipf and Stock Publishers
199 W. 8th Ave., Suite 3
Eugene, OR 97401

www.wipfandstock.com

ISBN 13: 978-1-60608-537-0

Cataloging-in-Publication data:

Heide, Gale.

    Domesticated glory : how the politics of America has tamed God / Gale Heide.

    xx + 162 p. ; 23 cm. Includes index(es).

    ISBN 13: 978-1-60608-537-0

    1. Christianity and politics. 2. Political theology. I. Title.

BR115.P7 H43 2010

Manufactured in the U.S.A.

To Trina and Alethia

Wisdom grows in pains of insight;
    Crafted slowly in the heart of the ear.
Days know no pace, nor years the schedule;
    Yet the moments cultivate judgment
    with hand-picked sympathy.

Growing is not always understanding;
    Interest requires suffering.
Pain your mind to give attention;
    Never reward the senses by fleeting memoirs.

Look to the height; favor the effort.
    Your heart's joy is in the rising.
Wait for discernment; seek sovereign view;
    Eyes familiar shall see.

Contents

Acknowledgments / ix

Introduction / xi

ONE   The Deceptive Allure of Home / 1

TWO   Finding Constantine: Evangelicals in the Politics of Postmodernism / 21

THREE   Faithful in Little ... The Primacy of Person in Biblical Truth / 44

FOUR   If these Become Silent, the Rocks Will Cry Out: The Public Nature of God's Glory / 67

FIVE   The Earth Is My Footstool: The Universal Politics of God's Honor! / 90

SIX   The Performance of a Lifetime: The Politics of Dying Well / 114

Subject Index / 151

Name Index / 155

Scripture Index / 157

Acknowledgments

I'VE NEVER LEARNED SO much as when I teach. Over the years of attempting to apprentice young minds into mature readers of Scripture, I've found that I am wonderfully transported from the lectern to the chair as I listen to them tease their way through difficult texts in the Old and New Testaments, Aristotle, Descartes, and Kant. It seems we rediscover the richness and meaning of reading all over again with each generation's successive moments of awakening to the reality of Jesus' Lordship over all creation and time. Hours of reading, thinking, and preparation suddenly seem worthwhile as faces express understanding and commitment.

The thoughts reflected in this work represent the culmination of several years of work. I first began thinking in the area of politics when introduced to the politics of the Gospel by teachers such as Bruce Ware and Gerry Breshears. Stanley Hauerwas later confronted and confounded many of the presuppositions I had always brought to the text of Scripture, freeing me to think more carefully about the politics of Jesus. With these foundations in place, I was "turned loose" by my college on unsuspecting students to challenge them to think more Biblically about themselves and the world. It is to this list I owe a great debt of thanks: my teachers for their careful consideration of my questions and my students for helping me continue to question the right things. The students who have helped me think better are too numerous to list, though they always seem to find their way into my philosophy and Bible classes.

Further, I owe Charlie Collier and Patrick Harrison a great debt for their patient work to make my thoughts understandable. I continually find that good writers are rare; most of us are resigned to constant revision. Consequently, I seek to become a good reviser. The work of good readers like Charlie and Patrick has made me a better writer and thinker.

The chapters below have been many years in the making. Over a decade ago, I sent versions of various chapters to several journals for consideration. The recurring theme in the responses was a hearty affirmation of the subject matter and approach but a fear over the repercussions of publishing such articles. The most telling response was "while we appreciate and agree with much of your article, we are not comfortable presenting it to our readership." With such guarded wisdom in mind, I have attempted to write in such a way as to draw attention to themes without unnecessarily offending. Nevertheless, I am certain I will offend many with my reflections on Scripture and the church. Hopefully, any offense can be limited to only those areas where offense could possibly be regarded as "necessary." Such an un-American notion as a necessary offense is admittedly dangerous. We may actually find ourselves in the midst of a disagreement. However, it has been my delight over the years to disagree with people I love and respect and remain good friends in the process. Friends like these are worth keeping.

As always, Mary and our girls, Trina and Alethia, have demonstrated Godly patience in the way they have sacrificed for the sake of producing another book. I offer them these pages as a gift that will hopefully endure beyond the things we could have done with the time spent writing. You are all very gracious in listening to my ideas and joining me in the contemplations and moldings that lead to belief. Any work I do or have done is as much from you as it is for you!

Introduction

I HAVE STOPPED COUNTING the number of bumper stickers I see each day proclaiming "God bless America" or some type of support for troops on foreign soil. I am not particularly critical of such slogans; in fact, I pray for America and her troops often. What is most interesting to me is the way in which Americans so easily presume that God has a vested interest in America. It seems an unquestioned assumption today, even by those who know their Bibles well, that God is somehow on the side of democracy. Such assumptions handicap God's supremacy, diminishing His own Lordship over the universe. Allow me to explain.

Human politics is always a difficult subject to discuss. Not because of various party commitments or economic ideologies, though they are cause for discord in their own right. It is specifically difficult because of the way in which politics is finally about our own hearts. Various beliefs we hold dear and the ways we wish to enforce them in our corner of the world are great cause for passion and preference, illustrating that politics is not finally about ideas. It is about life and how we believe it should be lived.

This is a book about politics and religion, though not written in the vein of how religion influences politics. I wish to discuss the more direct and indirect ways politics influences religion, or more specifically, Christianity. We will attempt to lay bare the underlying human issues that give rise to the exertion and manipulation of power. In other words, we will discuss politics at its root level—where beliefs intersect with social relationships. At this level, politics has much in common with religious belief, because the lines between them begin to blur. This is because when we are asked to address real issues in our world, politics often takes on religious overtones.

It is here, at the level of moral meaning and cultural control, that we find the greatest of conflicts occurring in our hearts, for it is here we find ourselves in an unending conflict with God. God has made political

Introduction

claims on our lives and the lives of others that trump all other claims. We wrestle against Him as we attempt to assert our own authority, but we are fighting a losing battle. Submission, or as Christians typically refer to it, conversion, is more than the mere recognition of this fact. Indeed, it is the embrace of His claims.

But America is, or at least it should be, unsettled by such far-reaching claims by God in the Bible. The lack of concern is likely due only to the fact that America has, thus far, been able to keep God "in His place." America has so privatized religion, making it primarily an issue of individual conscience, that God is now merely a matter of personal preference. Western politics undermines God's authority by proclaiming the supremacy of individual rights. In such a battle for supremacy, "What happens to God, or at least our conception of Him, when the power offered by the world becomes more attractive than He is?"

I have chosen to introduce us to the subject of human politics and God's glory by rehearsing a simple point from a sermon I first preached many years ago. At first glance, this point is strangely harsh to our ears. In fact, as I've pointed out this clear teaching of Scripture, it has caused some churches great discomfort with my preaching. In other words, I've not been invited back to these Bible-believing, conservative churches to speak again for fear of hearing further disquieting things from the Bible. However, it is a message we in America need to hear often. My intent is simply to draw attention to how our culture has coerced us to deny the supremacy of God in His plan for us and for the universe. God's plan in the Bible is to emphasize the supremacy of Jesus' Lordship over our lives. In contrast to this, the politics of America is slowly killing the centrality of Christ in Christian worship and devotion. And like the proverbial frog in the pot of ever-warming water, Christians are oblivious to what is happening each and every election year. Allow me to summarize this point from Scripture.

It is fairly commonplace now to admit that our American culture is centered around the self. We believe in the supremacy of self-interest to such an extent that all else is subjected to the question of personal gain. "What's in it for me?" is the measure of value placed on options posed to us. Even when we read the Bible, we read it as though God exists to cater to our every whim. We believe our personal destiny (i.e., salvation) is the central focus of Scripture. Such is the extent of our heresy.

Introduction

God lays claim to the lives of His followers in an all-encompassing manner. He leaves no doubt about who has control over the life of someone who wishes to be a disciple of Jesus. One might even go so far as to say God *owns* those who follow Him. Lest one might think I am conjecturing such a concept, consider the words of the apostle Paul in Rom 6:15–23.

> [15] What then? Shall we sin because we are not under law but under grace? May it never be! [16] Do you not know that when you present yourselves to someone as slaves for obedience, you are slaves of the one whom you obey, either of sin resulting in death, or of obedience resulting in righteousness? [17] But thanks be to God that though you were slaves of sin, you became obedient from the heart to that form of teaching to which you were committed, [18] and having been freed from sin, you became slaves of righteousness. [19] I am speaking in human terms because of the weakness of your flesh. For just as you presented your members as slaves to impurity and to lawlessness, resulting in further lawlessness, so now present your members as slaves to righteousness, resulting in sanctification. [20] For when you were slaves of sin, you were free in regard to righteousness. [21] Therefore what benefit were you then deriving from the things of which you are now ashamed? For the outcome of those things is death. [22] But now having been freed from sin and enslaved to God, you derive your benefit, resulting in sanctification, and the outcome, eternal life. [23] For the wages of sin is death, but the free gift of God is eternal life in Christ Jesus our Lord.

No middle ground exists for the Christian from which to determine one's own destiny. We are either slaves to sin or slaves to God. God has the right to direct the life of the Christian, and Christians have the obligation, no better, the delight to follow His wishes.

God has designed such a plan for human existence for purposes far higher than the benefit of individuals in their earthly or heavenly existence. In other words, His plans are not to cater to our own "life, liberty, and pursuit of happiness." His purposes are, since He really is God after all, centered on His own glory and honor. This is the great truth of God's New Covenant with His people, the church. He promised long ago that He would cause His people Israel to be a beacon of His honor. While that day still awaits its Jewish fulfillment, He is now accomplishing this same work through the church. This is how God words His plan through the prophet Ezekiel:

Introduction

> [22] Therefore say to the house of Israel, "Thus says the Lord GOD, It is not for your sake, O house of Israel, that I am about to act, but for My holy name, which you have profaned among the nations where you went. [23] I will vindicate the holiness of My great name which has been profaned among the nations, which you have profaned in their midst. Then the nations will know that I am the LORD," declares the Lord GOD, "when I prove Myself holy among you in their sight. [24] For I will take you from the nations, gather you from all the lands and bring you into your own land. [25] Then I will sprinkle clean water on you, and you will be clean; I will cleanse you from all your filthiness and from all your idols. [26] Moreover, I will give you a new heart and put a new spirit within you; and I will remove the heart of stone from your flesh and give you a heart of flesh. [27] I will put My Spirit within you and cause you to walk in My statutes, and you will be careful to observe My ordinances." (Ezek 36:22–27)

God's primary concern, and I think I learned this from Bruce Ware and John Piper, is His own glory and reputation. People are a means to that end, not ends in themselves. Allow me to state this as clearly as possible so my point is not missed: My individual right to choose my own destiny is a deception of Western democracy. This is not to deny the benefits of personal freedom, but perhaps we have confused the blessings with the curses that accompany individual freedom. In other words, "What happens to God when I believe I control my own world?"

Writing a book of this nature is always a risky business. It is so because I am critiquing widely beloved beliefs of western cultures. In the process of challenging political thoughts deeply embedded in the western mindset, I am also challenging some of the beliefs held dear by every American. The heritage of western democracy courses deep in the veins of traditional Americanism. But these are more than just the roots of western cultures. These are the roots of who we believe we are. Self-determination is the very basis for getting out of bed in the morning.

I do not wish to be dismissed as a liberal or postmodernist who simply does not value such notions as freedom and self-determination. Indeed, I recognize that without them I would not be able to write this book. (As a point of fact, I am actually taking a more literal/conservative stance on Scripture than those who laud human freedom as a necessity for existence.) Nevertheless, predispositions and presuppositions are never

Introduction

beyond examination, especially when it seems Christians have fallen out of line with Biblical teaching.

As we venture into the unseen world of our presuppositions and the hidden beliefs on which we base our lives, we should never make the mistake of assuming the infallibility of our own reason and rationality. I know my own tendency is to believe something to be true precisely because I believe it. This is a tendency that stems from our fallen human nature. What's more, political influences have glorified the self to such an extent that we now excuse such a tendency of human nature as the best way to know something.[1] Humility in the face of another way of thinking, even the authority of Scripture, is quickly set aside, since we have come to believe that our own way of thinking is most valid. Given the status of every individual as a rational creature operating on the same plane of ideas and self-determination, it is difficult for us to see the value of humility. However, as a Christian, I am not particularly interested in how to maintain humility in the face of warring ideas, though that may certainly be a subject worthy of consideration. Instead, I am asking a rather different question. I am asking about our humility in the face of God's revelation of Himself in word and person.

Obviously, interpretation becomes an issue, since not all agree on what Scripture says or how to understand the person of Jesus. However, we should all be able to loosen our grasp on our presuppositionss a bit when faced with the reality of the supreme God of the universe speaking clearly into our world. This is where western politics steps in and tells us to stand fast. It tells us to hold tightly to our autonomy and self-assurance, notions prominent in the American way, thereby challenging the very authority of God and His Word over our lives. Sometimes we do this without even knowing. My hope is that the church can be awakened to her deception and begin again a life that exhibits the Lordship of Jesus so clearly exalted in His Word.

Perhaps a better way to address how reading this book will impact a western mind is to imagine the plight of a world beyond our own. I am

---

1. René Descartes (1596–1650) believed the best method for discovering knowledge was through the rationality of the thinking self. His goal was to remove all of his teaching from his mind so his reason could arrive at conclusions without any influence or bias. Descartes' influence remains dominant in modern epistemology today, including many evangelical voices. See René Descartes, *Discourse on Method*, trans. by Donald Cress (Indianapolis: Hackett, 1993) paragraphs 12–15.

Introduction

not speaking of imagining the supernatural. Instead, I am speaking of the world of our brothers and sisters in Christ who see things very differently. Indeed, the lives of those who give everything for their faith are all too real and present in the church of today. The sad reality of martyrdom is discovered in countries far from the borders of English speaking governments. It is sad, not specifically because people are dying, though that should cause us pain and grief. The sadness is discovered more precisely in our pity. We feel like martyrdom is such a waste of life, when perhaps it is the best way to spend a life. Americans and other westerners believe we have moved beyond martyrdom with our notions of rights and freedom of belief. Unfortunately, the pluralistic nature of belief in such a world makes the beliefs themselves a mere matter of choice. In other words, belief in Jesus is now but another item on the menu, making it unworthy of death. It is but a preference. In light of such a smorgasbord of belief, the only thing left worth dying for is the right to have a choice. Such is the virtue of war in the West. We pity others for being denied such rights. It seems as though, perhaps, they see better than we do. We pray for their release and freedom; they pray for their own faithfulness and perseverance. We see a devastating loss; they see an indescribable gain.

Imagine a place where belief in Jesus is tantamount to a death sentence. Imagine a time when police beat and arrest you for professing Christ as Lord in opposition to claims of lordship by the government. Of course, we don't have to imagine. Such events are happening around us every day. The challenge to us is not to stop them. Jesus predicted the world would hate us, if we follow after Him (John 15:18–21). Our challenge is to be ready for them. We must pause and ask our heart of its own resolve in the face of rivaling challenges. The world has built many statues and asked us to bow at their feet. Like Daniel's friends, Shadrach, Meshach, and Abednego, we are being asked once again whom we will serve. We, in the West, have been lulled into a state where we no longer even hear the question of allegiance. We follow along blindly . . . deafly. Hopefully, the chapters below will make the question clear once again.

Chapter 1 delineates how the foundations of American politics are primarily anthropocentric. Human comfort and preservation are consistently offered as motivation and justification for rallying collective power. Much of current Christian engagement with the political world reveals a latent anthropocentrism within western evangelicalism. While disagreeing with other political ideologies over the methodology to accomplish

Introduction

their utopic vision for humanity's future (e.g., socialism), general agreement exists as to the purpose of political power: the better life. The doctrinal expression in Christianity of American anthropocentrism is seen most clearly within evangelicalism in the current trend toward a postmillennial understanding of the "Kingdom of God." It is on this point of the millennial kingdom having begun that America becomes a "Christian nation."

In the second chapter, the discussion of political ideological commitments continues with specific attention given to the Biblical defense offered by evangelicals for such commitments. The anthropocentric nature of a democratic ideology is tied directly to its Enlightenment heritage, demonstrating the anthropological and theological compromise made by evangelicals with the liberal theology spawned by Enlightenment thought. The Enlightenment turn to individual autonomy adopted into the founding documents of the United States highlights modernity's exaltation of humanity to a level rivaling God's own claims to sovereignty discovered in Scripture.

The next chapter outlines how the truth wars between subjectivists (truth is subject to my own interpretive context) and absolutists (truth resides in statements of knowledge as they correspond to reality) are in fact a debate couched in terms not regarded as important to the Biblical authors. The battle for truth is often centered on statements that will gain footing in the field of secular control, i.e., the public square. Those who hold to absolute truth (i.e., foundationalists) attempt to secure a rationally defensible position clear to all who observe it—believer and nonbeliever alike. However, the foundation for knowledge in Scripture is not centered in philosophical defenses; it is centered on the person of Jesus. The Biblical authors are more concerned with "What is faithful to the life of Jesus?" This demonstrates that discussions of truth in Scripture are primarily centered on the character of people formed into the image of Christ. Truth is about being truthful, not an abstract notion available to any rational mind. In other words, truth is not egalitarian, as supposed by moderns, both subjectivists and objectivists alike. Universal, or absolute, truth is primarily a theological, even revelational issue, not a rational one. More in line with Jesus' claim to be the truth, we should be asking the question "Who is the Truth?" rather than "What is the truth?"

No discussion of American politics and religion would be complete without some analysis of the founders' intentions. Chapter 4 introduces

Introduction

readers to the goals behind Thomas Jefferson's documentation of religious freedoms and rights. The impact of Jefferson's Virginia Act for Establishing Religious Freedom on the later writing of the First Amendment to the US Constitution is examined from the perspective of the American impulse to privatize religion. Jefferson's desire to subject religion to individual conscience is a direct contrast to the Biblical emphasis on the public nature of God's glory. Privatization of religion and the American tendency toward pluralism, stemming specifically from the language of the First Amendment, leaves God's glory to the preference of the individual. Scripture makes clear the plan of God to extend His fame to the ends of the earth and make His name supreme over all creation. America's freedom of religion is finally but another attempt to drown out God's glory in the din of pluralism. In contrast, Scripture compels Christians not to be silenced by political demands for personal preference.

John Piper has reminded the evangelical community of its foundation and purpose by heralding the biblical theme of God's glory. Chapter 5 indicates how this theme has been eclipsed in the last few centuries due to the rise of humanity's glorification of the self. Though glorification of the self has been a central motif in human history since the Fall, the individual autonomy of the Enlightenment has further entrenched and justified humanity's inflated estimation of its own value within the Biblical paradigm. In contrast, Scripture subjects all things to the purpose of magnifying God's reputation. Colossians 1:19–20 and Philippians 2:5–11 demonstrate that the reconciliation of all things through the cross of Christ means every created thing discovers its value and purpose within the movement of God to draw all things unto Himself. Nothing can alter or escape His efforts. Even the enemies of God are reconciled for the sake of finally establishing the kingship of God over all. He not only defeats His enemies, He causes them to become subjects for worship of Himself.

The final chapter develops how the meaning of human existence is discovered as humans participate in the expression of God's glory. Human relationship is the primary means for this display, especially as humans function as the body of Christ. In other words, the created purpose for humanity is defined as Christocentric, not anthropocentric. Christian witness (i.e., the performance of the Scriptures) is the most political activity in which we can engage as humans. The rationality of witness, particularly the witness of martyrdom, only makes sense in a Christocentric theology. The nature of death and its influence in American culture illustrates the politics involved in living with the knowledge that death is inescapable. Paul's placement of Romans 13 (how to live with government) in the context of Romans 12 (how to live with those who are in opposition) serves to provide believers with a training manual for embracing the witness to the state provided by martyrdom.

God will settle for nothing less than the highest position of power and authority. This is a political claim that undermines and supersedes all other claims to authority, even the individual's belief in autonomy. Such a God is dangerous for the people who recognize Him as Lord. After all, He is a challenge to any and every other king. "Who are we in America that we have forgotten the danger He poses?" For us, God is no longer so dangerous. Indeed, America believes it has domesticated God!

ONE

The Deceptive Allure of Home

GOD'S REPUTATION IS PARAMOUNT in His purposes for all of human history. Scripture seems clear that humanity is a means to such an end. Theologians and the church at large seemed to have embraced such a notion for centuries. People understood the mighty hand of God over their lives and well-being. The human circumstance has changed, especially in recent centuries. In a matter of decades, medical advances and the rise of first-world status for much of the west has given confidence to humans formerly existing under the curses of plagues and poverty. Human optimism has grown alongside these advances over the last two centuries. Vowing never to return to the "dark days" of past wars and abuses, many triumph in the Hegelian belief that humans are reaching the pinnacle of their existence.

One should hardly bemoan the loss of past centuries when death surrounded daily existence and the future was far from predictable. No one would wish for a return to the pre-industrial days of constant labor and the seemingly whimsical nature of death. However, it seems a certainty that the betterment of the human condition, and the incumbent boost in optimism, has led humanity away from a consistent awareness of God's providence. What's more, humanity in the west can now easily dismiss any claims of authority by God over human history, when humans are so confident in the control each individual has over his or her destiny. God may be made a partner in the human endeavor, but in the mind of modern man, He is hardly the master of anyone.

One of the more significant ways in which we see evangelical Christians embracing fundamental beliefs that draw them away from their commitment to Biblical notions like God's authority and ultimate glory is in their allegiance to the success of the political experiment associated specifically with America's republican government. American

Christians often seem so devoted to American ideology that God's glory, for American Christians, becomes suddenly wed to the success of America. As we begin our conversation about Christian political involvement, it is critical to focus our discussion to a few salient points. Involvement in political activities is not what's at issue. Instead, it is the confidence placed in human politics that challenges God's supremacy over human history. We are far too "at home" in this world. Certain fundamental beliefs about citizenship and the inherent rights associated with such citizenship betray a level of commitment to ideologies that may not be as compatible with Christianity as Constantinian presumption (i.e., that Christians are still living in Christendom) has led us to believe. I am not intending to engage in a diatribe against one particular political party or another in America. Indeed, both of the dominant parties display a rampant liberalism in their understanding of anthropology, individual liberties, individual rights, and autonomy. A simple quote by one party representative should demonstrate the widely held commitment to individual autonomy: "The largest promise of the democratic idea is that, given the right to govern themselves, free men and women will prove to be the best stewards of their own destiny."[1] It would be, put quite simply, illegitimate to argue the comparative qualities of liberalism between Republicans or Democrats. At a foundational level, both display commitments to human optimism and a commitment to human control of history that easily overshadows the Biblical commitment of laying down any so-called "rights" for the sake of witness or trusting in God's providence. Of course, such a discussion undermines the question of *how* the church should relate to politics, since I believe the prior issue of who we are as Christians needs to be addressed. As will be demonstrated below, the evangelical church has, at times, embraced a political ideology that is detrimental to the display of God's glory. God's glory is best displayed in our existence as church, which is a political community that takes precedence over our existence in the world. Unfortunately, rather than seeing its own existence as political,

---

1. Al Gore, *Earth in the Balance: Ecology and the Human Spirit* (New York: Plume, 1992) 276. Both Republicans and Democrats generally agree with the Enlightenment notion that education is able to accomplish moral achievements rivaling conversion. Further, individual autonomy and the notion of rights are a shared assumption for success by both parties.

The Deceptive Allure of Home

in that it displays the Lordship of Jesus daily, the church has typically joined itself with the political processes of the world.[2]

It is becoming clearer every election year that certain branches of the church in America believe they have a stake in seeing America succeed. In other words, to put the matter in more theological terms, many American evangelicals and fundamentalists are returning to the belief that America is God's "new heaven and new earth" realized. Human welfare in the West is now almost solely subject to the success of the priests of power in the arena of political struggle. Obviously, Christians still pray for God's intervention, but His help is primarily requested as an assurance for the direction of those humans involved in providing guidance to temporal affairs. As the search for a Christian America continues, the primitivist tendency true of most "New Testament" churches elides easily with the repristination of a purer America.[3] The campaign to "Take Back America"

---

2. Even the good work of Russell D. Moore in his *Kingdom of Christ: The New Evangelical Perspective* (Wheaton: Crossway, 2004) still suffers from the presumption of politics as power within the world's system. Moore does a fantastic job of tracing the historical discussions of Kingdom interpretations and their relationship to eschatology and politics in the west. Unfortunately, he remains convinced, as was Carl Henry, that the only two options are engagement or isolation (e.g., 66–67). Although he rightly develops a robust understanding of the relationship between church and Kingdom, even to the point of arguing for the necessity of ecclesial priority in political engagement, he still seems to equate socio-political engagement with specific political activities of power and influence *within* the world's political processes. One is left wondering how such engagement could possibly happen in China or Indonesia. This leads me to believe that ecclesiology is being paid mere lip service and is not the primary social community for which Moore is searching. The church *as* politics, though perhaps seen in theoretical constructions, bears little meaning for Moore when it comes to real issues of power and control. Being the church still comes down to having the numbers to accomplish legislation (cf. his lament over fragmentation in evangelicalism on 175ff.).

For Moore, and others who would understand the Kingdom along such lines, the focus seems skewed toward the human element in construction of the Kingdom. While certainly humans will play a role in the Kingdom, one is left wondering as to its purpose. In other words, why have a Kingdom at all? Theologically, those who focus on the "already" nature of human history, more specifically American history, seem centered too heavily on anthropology as the hub of Christian doctrine. Christology seems once again to be overshadowed by concerns for human destiny. In such scenarios, the Kingdom is finally for mere human welfare.

3. I received a publication of the Christian Defense Fund entitled *One Nation Under God: America's Christian Heritage* (Springfield, VA: Christian Defense Fund, 1997). One of the more interesting things I was afforded by this publication was the section on Thomas Jefferson. To my surprise, it seems Jefferson is now to be regarded as one of the defenders of authentic "fundamental" Christian faith as it intertwines with democratic ideologies

and its ensuing cultural war appears to be designed specifically to make the world a safe place in which to be a Christian.[4] Those "liberals" who are attempting to remove religion from public life, e.g., those who oppose a God who creates, prayer in school and the word "God" in the pledge of allegiance, must be pushed back so that Christianity can once again flourish in the public arena.[5] The fight is one that is waged in the realm of religious freedom and the "right" to free speech. Therefore, legislation must be secured that protects and promotes the religious values that were seemingly shared by all generations of Americans until as late as the 1950s.[6]

(29–32). Given his disdain for any sense of the supernatural (e.g., the Jefferson Bible), I suspect he would also be surprised to find himself in such a work.

4. It is no mere coincidence that a growing branch of Focus on the Family's ministry is the Alliance Defense Fund, a "ministry" to defend believers against legal assaults. Imagine what the martyrs through the centuries could have done, if only they could have had lawyers.

5. Interestingly, these liberals seem to resemble the dreaded "communists" of the last generation's cultural war. I wonder sometimes if American Christianity is inherently dualistic in that it always needs an enemy to survive. Thus, the material/physical existence of the church always appears as an antithesis to the materiality of the prevailing culture (e.g., the way Christians dress, wear their hair, etc. is often supported by the phrase, "We don't want to look like the world!"). Even Christian ethics is often discovered only as a reaction to the world's promotion of certain free expressions. This seems to be what drives evangelical ethics to constantly focus on issues rather than existence, on choices rather than character.

Perhaps, such a parasitic existence is what one gets when the definition of "church" is left at the theoretical level. The only real existence (i.e., physical or material presence) the church has come to know is a type of Pharisaical existence in that we know what we're against (e.g., abortion, homosexuality, etc.)—"Thou shalt not . . .", but no one really knows what the church is for. Thus, Christians are easily ensnared by the coerciveness of other gods: Americanism, and the inherent legalism associated with it, being a good example. Where is the material existence of a community that heralds the supremacy of God? This is politics in a different voice.

6. Cf. Ramesh Ponnuru, "Secularism and Its Discontents," *National Review* (December 27, 2004). I have avoided citing any one work or figure to this point for two reasons. First, I believe it is fairly apparent that this is a common ethos of many different groups and people who are advocating a "return to a Christian America," or better, "a return to modern Constantinianism." Second, I do not wish to single out any one group as a lone voice in the movement. These are broadly shared sentiments, especially at the grass roots level in many congregations. I will spend some time in this study focusing on published comments by James Dobson's *Focus on the Family* and branches of the ministry with which he is associated, but I hardly consider his work a singular cause in the movement. Rather, his position is merely one of the most popular and is well articulated in his publications. He also provides a good discussion partner in that he wishes, at least to my knowledge, to remain pre-millennial. Others (e.g., James Kennedy, Pat Robertson) in the Americanist

The Deceptive Allure of Home

In a context such as this, the question that seems glaringly obvious is, "What would happen to the church if America failed?" In other words, "Where would the church in America be if all her liberties were lost?" To state this in a more theological context, "What has happened to pre-millennialism? Where has the belief that we are 'between the times' gone?"[7] Even more to the point, "Is God's glory necessarily linked to the success of America, or any other culture, for that matter?" Before I deal with the answers I expect from those who would attempt to reconcile pre-millennialism with a strong patriotism (e.g., that government is a necessary evil, so we might as well make the most of it), allow me to state

---

movement have already declared their post-millennial sentiments. (It is not coincidental that with his growing interest in politics Pat Robertson seems to have left behind any pre-millennial commitments he once had in favor of a post-millennial perspective on America.)

I wish to make it clear that any criticism aimed at Dobson could just as easily be directed toward a number of groups clamoring after the same cause (e.g., Christian Coalition, Moral Majority, etc.). The critique offered here could also be aimed at preterists who believe the destructiuon of Jerusalem in 70 AD constituted the end of God's promises to Israel as a nation. For them, the church is the new Israel, making any promises to Israel applicable only to the church. Reconstruction of God's kingdom in America is the logical conclusion from such an interpretation. However, such a depiction of God's activity puts arbitrary limits on Him. Further, reconstructionism seems to stem from a preference for interpreting the Bible according to one cultural institutionalization of the church over Israel. This seems to be the same mistake once made by Roman Catholicism in its conception of the church's hegemony over history. While God's activity with the church may be His preference for a time, that does not imply an eternal shift in His promises, nor does it seem a license for control.

By dealing with a mere fraction of the literature on this subject, and only one group's work at that, I do not wish to be unfair or unscholarly. If I opened the floodgate, it may be impossible to exhaust all the material and groups. I have chosen a small bit of one as representative. If I were to attempt to substantiate every point for every group, I fear I would cloud the reader from seeing the forest for the sake of all the trees. I am quite open to being proven wrong regarding the popular sentiments among the majority of evangelicals and fundamentalists, and I am willing to critically engage thinkers in this regard. What I wish to do in these pages is merely reflect on some ideas that are intended as fodder for further discussion. I will leave it to the reader to decide if I have accurately portrayed our current situation.

7. I am very intrigued by the theological possibilities discussed by Moore as he attempts to find a middle ground between dispensationalists and covenant theologians regarding the reality of the kingdom in the present age. While I find his "already—not yet" development of the notion of kingdom helpful, particularly as he associates it with ecclesiology, he still seems to suffer from a thin definition of church. See Moore, *Kingdom of Christ*, 147–73.

this more clearly in Biblical terminology: "How would the apostles Paul and Peter view the Americanist movement?"

PILGRIMAGE OR PLANTATION?

When the apostle Peter wrote to his readers, it is quite apparent that he assumed they had no political influence. This is not to say that they were apolitical, but that the politics of the church was something vastly different from the politics of the world. When he addresses them as "aliens" or "sojourners" (παρεπιδημοις) in 1 Pet 1:1; 2:11, little doubt should remain in our minds as to their status in the lands to which they had scattered. They were foreigners within the various regions Peter lists in 1 Pet 1:1. But their status as aliens is not limited merely to their nationality or language. The difference extends even to the level of ontology (i.e., who they are). Indeed, Peter goes on to say in 1 Pet 2:11–12 that they should continue to regard themselves as strangers and use their position *qua strangers* to demonstrate the difference or gap that exists between themselves and the Gentiles—between Christians and the world. Thus, Peter leaves little room for Christians to become engaged with the world on the world's terms, as if the world could be made more like the church. He wishes for them to use their status as strangers to draw people out of the world and into a different realm of reality—that of the church. His is not a message of trying to find middle ground or a lowest common denominator with the world so that we can all live in peace. Indeed, such a translation of Christianity into neutral language presents the world with a Christianity that is no longer Christian. Nor is he advocating an attempt to take over the world so that righteousness will prevail. Instead, he is advocating conversion, even if Christians are killed to demonstrate what living in this other world means. In other words, though Peter is no masochist, he hardly advocates the priority of making the world a safe place in which to be a Christian. He expects trials and mistreatment will come (1 Pet 2:12, 20–23). His instruction is not to escape by reforming culture, but to endure in a manner that is conspicuous. His presupposition is always one of a different sort of political power: witness instead of control. Even as Christ "kept entrusting Himself to Him who judges rightly" (2:23), so we are to live a witness that places our destiny and safety in the hands of the Lord.

The Deceptive Allure of Home

This is a different sort of trust than to what we have grown accustomed. We tend to think of safety as being free from any threat of harm, whether real or supposed. However, God calls us to trust Him and follow His lead wherever that may take us. It may not be a safe road, but it will always be the best one to follow. I am reminded of C. S. Lewis's inquisitive children in *The Lion, The Witch, and the Wardrobe*. In their discussion with Mr. and Mrs. Beaver about meeting Aslan, the children are surprised He is a lion.

> "Ooh!" Said Susan, "I'd thought he was a man. Is he—quite safe? I shall feel rather nervous about meeting a lion."
> "That you will, dearie, and no mistake," said Mrs. Beaver, "if there's anyone who can appear before Aslan without their knees knocking, they're either braver than most or else just silly."
> "Then he isn't safe?" said Lucy.
> "Safe?" said Mr. Beaver. "Don't you hear what Mrs. Beaver tells you? Who said anything about safe? 'Course he isn't safe. But he's good. He's the King I tell you."[8]

Life with God is rarely safe, but we can rely on the fact that His way will always lead to our greatest good and His greatest glory, even when it hurts or results in our death.

I fear perhaps we in America have made an idol out of safety and security. Safety may not seem an idol, but just imagine if our safety were challenged. We believe we have the right to be secure and safe, even during one of the most dangerous activities in which we can engage: corporate worship. Were we to lose safety during corporate worship, what would happen to the church? Would we as the church go so far as to kill for the sake of maintaining peace and order in worship? Are we really so attached to life and a particular lifestyle in this world?

The apostle Paul took a different approach when it came to how the church should engage the world. His politics was of a different order from the world's. Even his prayer in 1 Tim 2:1–2 does not necessitate a binding of the Christian's plight to political preferences:

> First of all then I urge that entreaties and prayers, and petitions and thanksgivings be made on behalf of all men, for kings and all who are in authority, in order that we may lead a tranquil and quiet life in all godliness and dignity (or seriousness).

---

8. C. S. Lewis, *The Lion, the Witch and the Wardrobe* (New York: Collier, 1950) 75–76.

Paul's prayer indicates a definite preference for peace and an uninterrupted existence for the church, something all could agree is preferable. However, he does not indicate here a decided effort for accomplishing this peace outside of praying for it and trusting in God's sovereignty. It would be hermeneutically impossible to understand this passage as somehow granting the Christian warrant for establishing peace through the acquisition of kingship or control. If our welfare was finally up to us, then why pray? On this point, it is interesting to note that Paul here advocates prayers for *all* those in authority, not just "our" authorities. When was the last time we prayed for the kings and authorities of other countries (besides America's allies)? Paul moves directly from his prayer for a "quiet life" to instructions on how to function as the church (1 Tim 2:8ff.), indicating his concern that we *pray* for governmental leaders and we *work* to establish the church. These are two very different activities focused on two divergent kingdoms, though both will hopefully serve the ultimate purpose of establishing the honor of the Lord's name in all people and nations (1 Tim 2:3–5). But is it the Christian's responsibility to see His honor established in both kingdoms?

Focusing again on personal welfare and safety, surely one might object that Paul evidenced a high regard for nationalism through his use of his own Roman citizenship in the book of Acts. On the other hand, it must be remembered that Paul appealed to Caesar not for leniency or for the sake of "fair" treatment. Rather, his appeal was intended to provide him with an audience in Rome to which he might witness (Acts 23:11; 25:11—the order of these passages is important). Though Paul may seem to be preserving his life in Acts 25:11, in fact it does not appear as though he ever believes his life is his own (e.g., Phil 2:21–26; 2 Tim 4:6–8). Instead of attempting to preserve his existence, Paul knows that he is intended to go to Rome (Acts 23:11) and manipulates the situation to effect the journey. Even further with regard to Paul's commitment to national citizenship, his entreaty to obey those in authority (Rom 13) is stretched beyond all hermeneutical tensions if it is somehow understood as a command to wrest the reins of control from those we simply don't want in power or to change the laws so that we might somehow be treated more fairly. We mustn't forget that the same government to which Paul made his appeal in Acts and which he told the Romans to obey is also the government that killed him and many of his friends. (If one dates the writing of Romans in the late 50's, Nero is already emperor when Paul states his teaching

The Deceptive Allure of Home

regarding submitting to authorities in Romans 13. Please notice that Paul never printed a retraction when Nero turned on the Christians.) In other words, Paul's goal was never self-preservation or the societal welfare of those who called themselves Christian. Since Christians, of all people, know that suffering (e.g., unfair treatment) and death are not our final enemies and should not be feared (Matt 10:24–33; 2 Tim 3:12), we should not seek somehow to shelter ourselves from the witness they can provide.[9] Indeed, the author of Hebrews seems to recommend that a spirit of joy accompany unfair treatment, "For you showed sympathy to the prisoners, and accepted joyfully the seizure of your property, knowing that you have for yourselves a better possession and an abiding one" (Heb 10:34).

The notion that government is a "necessary evil" to control anarchy and subdue evil seems, at first glance, to be in line with what Paul has in mind in Romans 13 and 1 Tim 2:1–4.[10] However, it is an unwarranted leap to say that since this is the case, Christians should be the ones in control of the government, or even have a stake in helping it succeed. Nicholas Wolterstorff has outlined a defense of Christian participation in which he understands Paul to be speaking abstractly in Romans 13; Paul is speaking

---

9. What this means for those who would wish to sway public opinion or control the reins of the executive, legislative, or judicial branches of government in America is that they are fighting in the wrong arena. Instead of trying to make the world look more like the church, they should be working to make the church a place where people are willing to be mistreated and die for the sake of testifying to the Lordship of Jesus. This was the witness of the first several centuries of the church (until 313—the Edict of Milan); and by their deaths they testified to an opposing reality more effectively than perhaps any generation since.

How odd it is that American Christians should be willing to kill for the sake of protecting religious security (i.e., religious freedom) while their brothers and sisters around the world are discovering the power of their testimony through death on account of the Lordship of Jesus. If one of the earliest marks of the difference between heresy and orthodoxy in the early church was whether one was willing to be martyred for his/her set of beliefs, the American church would be highly suspect by this point in our history.

10. This is, though he may not like the wording, Calvin's take on the purpose of human government. See John Calvin, *Institutes of the Christian Religion*, ed. by John T. McNeill, trans. by Ford Lewis Battles (Philadelphia: Westminster, 1960) 4.20.1–32. Calvin was by no means opposed to human government, since it was ordained by God. He provides Scriptural basis for both its existence and its workings, and gives preferences for how wisdom might best be discovered by those in power. However, he seems apprehensive in these sections to proclaim it to be the task of the church to be responsible for it, and for good reason, having just left Roman Catholicism's earthly understanding of the Kingdom of God behind. Rather, he simply supports the Christian's obedience to the government that is in place.

"normatively and not descriptively."[11] Wolterstorff believes the political climate for Christians at this time under Nero was predominantly peaceful, thus Paul could outline a generic understanding of the relationship of Christians to government. Wolterstorff admits such a belief is a presumption; however, he fails to recognize the coercive power of any state government, aimed as it is at the common good of all citizens.[12] Early Christianity's drive to serve a King who challenged the authority of the state (i.e., Jesus) makes it difficult to imagine a space in which state (especially the Roman empire) and church can cohabitate without constant antagonism, at least, this side of the physical reign of Christ. Wolterstorff recognizes this problem and attempts to make a case for the state as an extension of Christ's authority. "Not only is Christ the head of the church. In this present era, it is not God the Father but Christ whose authority is mediated by the state."[13] While this seems an appealing answer to the relationship of church to state, such a post-millennial perspective is historically naïve. The question for Wolterstorff is, obviously, "Which state government?" Presumably, Wolterstorff would respond by directing our submission toward whichever one expresses and maintains God's justice consistently. Though a case may be made that America does this, it seems to be a steadily weakened case. I'm not sure Wolterstorff's argument is a theological development of the state from Romans 13 so much as it is a theological justification of America based in a presumptive history of justice. Where would Wolterstorff's understanding of the state be if, in the final analysis, Islamic countries were found to express justice more consistently and reverently than America? In other words, Wolterstorff's argument only works if we presuppose a commitment to the success of a specific state, which is something Wolterstorff himself recognizes Paul could not do.[14]

Even Martin Luther's two worlds theory doesn't warrant a commitment to the powers available in the political arena.[15] Luther was severely

---

11. Nicholas Wolterstorff, "Theological Foundations for an Evangelical Political Philosophy," *Toward an Evangelical Public Policy* (Grand Rapids: Baker, 2005) 148.

12. Ibid., 156.

13. Ibid., 151.

14. Ibid., 156.

15. By focusing on Luther's theory of two worlds, I am not attempting to ignore Augustine's two cities. I simply recognize that Luther was making use of Augustine and has greater bearing on modern politics in the church than Augustine. Further, Augustine's

opposed to those who believed the church should establish the government for the world. Initially, he seemed like a supporter of the post-millennial "chiliasts" who championed the building of God's kingdom on earth. As Oberman makes clear,

> Initially, Martin Luther was well received among chiliasts. They welcomed him as a prophet of transition to a new era and defender of the "new age," the age of the Spirit and of peace. But he disappointed them, for his reformation did not seek to transform society in order to prepare the way for the millennium. Bitterly, the militant "champions of God" turned away from him. Preeminent among them was Thomas Münzer, who had a large following of chiliast prophets, all of them driven by the will to extirpate the "godless" in order to ensure that the reformation would be in place in time for the Day of Judgment.[16]

Luther had just left a church that saw itself as the kingdom of God on earth.[17] He was hardly in a mood to join with those who wished to establish a new kingdom. To push our original point further, Luther saw no problem with Christians serving in the state government, as long as they did so as Christians and never had to compromise their primary commitment to Jesus. However, he had no expectations that such a service to the world would somehow change the world. Rather such service to the world was merely an outgrowth of the life-changing faith and love of neighbor every Christian had growing within them. Serving in the government was an act of service to one's neighbors. If the government became corrupt, the service was not to change into revolution. One's only recourse was to "witness, pray, and suffer."[18] One may think that perhaps Luther's concep-

---

proximity to Constantine and the political revolution in the church during his era seem to have left the church during the Dark Ages with little other option than post-millennialism. Luther is trying to find a way out from under this.

16. Heiko A. Oberman, *Luther: Man between God and the Devil*, trans. by Eileen Walliser-Schwarzbart (New York: Image, 1992) 60–61.

17. Ibid., 64. Oberman delineates Luther's opposition to those "Zionists" who take matters into their own hands regarding the establishment of God's kingdom on earth. To be fair to the pre-Luther church, we must recognize that not all believed the Kingdom of God was an external reality discovered in Roman Catholicism. See Avery Dulles, "The Spiritual Community of Man: The Church according to Saint Thomas," in *Calgary Aquinas Studies*, ed. by Anthony Parel (Toronto: Pontifical Institute of Mediaeval Studies, 1978) 133.

18. David C. Steinmetz, *Luther in Context* (Bloomington: Indiana University Press, 1986) 124.

tion of the two governments of God (church and state) implies that, at the least, one could expect God's reign to be seen on a smaller scale in places where His church was more predominant. However, Luther never believed such could be the case. Summarizing Luther's thought on the subject, Hagen concludes:

> Since, however, the whole world is evil and that among thousands there is scarcely one true Christian . . . it is out of the question that there should be a common Christian government over the whole world, or indeed over one land or company of people, since the wicked always outnumber the good.[19]

Instead of taking over or becoming isolationistic, Luther had a view of Christians involved in the world in a more prophetic/evangelistic manner. The best thing the church can do for the world is not pacify it in its own moral ineptitude, nor try to shape the world into a sub-Christian pseudo-church. The best thing the church can do for the world is to let it know it is the world, so that it might see its need for the forgiveness and redemption found in Jesus. This is hardly an apolitical position, but neither is it a full engagement with the world on the world's terms. Just as we are not called to bury our heads in the sand, likewise Luther believes, we are not called to try to "out-world" the world.[20]

---

19. Kenneth Hagen, "Luther's Doctrine of the Two Kingdoms," *Reformation & Revival Journal* 7 (1998) 117. Hagen is here referring to comments made by Luther in his work *Temporal Authority* (see *Luther's Works*, vol. 45, ed. by Walther I. Brandt [Philadelphia: Fortress, 1962] 89).

20. Though I'm not sure he would agree with my interpretation of Luther's "two worlds," the language in my description of Luther is heavily influenced by Stanley Hauerwas's understanding of the relationship of the church to the world. Hauerwas is fond of stating in many of his works that the role of the church is to be the church so that the world might know it is the world. For a good example of this statement with some contextual development, see Stanley Hauerwas, *The Peaceable Kingdom* (Notre Dame: University of Notre Dame Press, 1983) 99–102. Cf. Stanley Hauerwas, *Wilderness Wanderings: Probing Twentieth-Century Theology and Philosophy* (Boulder, CO: Westview, 1997) 2–3; and Stanley Hauerwas, *Character and the Christian Life: A Study in Theological Ethics* (San Antonio: Trinity University Press, 1975) 223.

One wonders if Hauerwas's church needs the world in order to exist. One might question whether he in fact holds a dualistic or antithetical view of the church–world relation. Hauerwas would likely respond that this is simply what it's like to be "between the times." What the church is experiencing is the "already–not yet" aspect of the Kingdom of God—we are already under the umbrella of the "kingdom of God," but it has not yet been fully realized on earth. As such, the church cannot help but struggle to maintain and build its identity, particularly in the face of such tempting assimilation as that offered by

The Deceptive Allure of Home

One final comment on Paul's perspective seems necessary before we leave the heritage of the apostolic relationship to politics in the world. In Romans 13, Paul echoes Jesus's command to "render to Caesar the things that are Caesar's and to God the things that are God's" (Matt 22:15–22). Paul seems to be saying that a peaceable witness is preferred to one that requires our death (Paul, like Peter, also does not advocate masochism—cf. 1 Tim 2:1–2), but if the latter is what it takes, then to God be the glory— Paul's life is not his own. In contrast, there are many today who believe that "freedom must exist if the church is to flourish."[21] There seems to be a melding of the thoughts in Romans 13 with a Constantinian compulsion to control in such a way that Christians in America are prone to think of the government in Romans 13 as "us" instead of "them." Many American evangelicals have come to believe that God's ordination of the government in Romans 13 means its purpose necessarily parallels that of the church. We have forgotten that nations in the Old Testament were likewise "ordained" by God for varying purposes, including the judgment and punishment of God's own people. It seems extremely unlikely that Paul's recognition of the Roman government as ordained by God would also have been interpreted by his audience as a Christianization of Romanism. Such an understanding of the passage would have created great confusion when the Roman government started killing Christians in larger num-

---

the world. Hauerwas would go even further to say that this is why patience is a key virtue for the church in its contemporary context. The church is now in a context in which hope should be its "mode of being." The temptation for Christians is to "set up" or "build" the Kingdom in the world. The church does not have the patience to wait for Christ to establish His Kingdom. But in fact, that is the reality in which the church finds, or should find, itself. The church is waiting for the eschatological Kingdom, and until that day, we are called to continue as a distinct witness to the life, death, and resurrection of Jesus. See Hauerwas, *Peaceable Kingdom*, 101–6.

21. Tom Minnery, "The Relationship between Church, Family and Government," *Focus on the Family* (July, 1998) 11. Minnery, among others, believes that a necessary link exists between a peaceful society and the success of the Gospel, interpreting Paul's words to Timothy in 1 Tim 2:1-4 to be a direct confirmation that the Gospel cannot flourish without peace. Of course, what Minnery's position ignores (and Minnery himself even contradicts in the same article) is that Paul's was not a peaceful society, nor was the history of the church for the first few centuries one of peace. Peace was certainly desirable, but it was not necessary. The Gospel seemed to get along just fine, even flourished, in the midst of adversity. In fact, though problems obviously existed, most evangelicals/fundamentalists would argue that the church was most pure and on the right track during Paul's day. Ultimately, what Minnery's position portrays is a belief that death or suffering is somehow the final enemy, to be avoided at almost any cost.

bers for their faith. Indeed, the ancient literature lacks any such confusion. Nowhere do Paul or the apostles who survived him, nor the early church Fathers, offer any evidence that they expected an earthly government to arise alongside the church to promote the supremacy of Christ on earth. Instead, they awaited the return of Christ to establish His own kingdom and authority. As Paul notes to the Philippians, "For our citizenship is in heaven, from which also we *eagerly wait* for a Savior, the Lord Jesus Christ . . ." (Phil 3:20; emphasis mine).

Paul's plea in Romans 13 is one of humble submission to the government. Influences today outside the Biblical text have led evangelical politicians to the conclusion that this passage somehow prescribes an active stance toward engagement *on the same plane* with the world's politics. In other words, we seem to have concluded that a specific expression of the world's government is now the ideal parallel to the church's commission to establish the supremacy of Christ in her midst. To those who would subscribe to such a belief the question must be posed, "When did the church become married to the notions of freedom and democracy?"[22]

THE DEATH OF PRE-MILLENNIALISM?

Pre-millennialism, in its many different forms, has always maintained that God's kingdom would be established by Christ at some point in the future and no one or nothing could hasten that event through the establishment of some pre-kingdom. Likewise, pre-millennialism has always taught that the church is "between the times." In other words, our existence is as

---

22. Dobson (James Dobson, "Family News From Dr. James Dobson," *Focus on the Family* [June, 1999] 2–3) seems to confuse confrontation with commitment in his defense of "the historic posture of the church . . . Down through the ages, godly leaders have confronted wicked regimes and their policies." While it is true that confrontation with political leaders and their policies is a common occurrence in the church, Dobson has not answered the question as to whether the church has rightly engaged the public realm through the centuries (e.g., Constantinianism), nor has he addressed the issue of whether confrontation constitutes making a commitment to devising a better social order for the world. Confronting wickedness is something different from taking over. The prophets are a good example in this regard in that they were constantly speaking against the unrighteousness of governing authorities, both Jews and non-Jews. But speaking against powers and wresting the reins of control from them are two different things. Dobson has confused the role of the prophet and the role of the king. Prophecy accomplishes righteousness in a manner quite different from that of conquest, and often such righteousness is discovered in witness, even the witness of isolation and death. Prophets functioned in a far different way than kings in the Old Testament.

pilgrims or sojourners—aliens in a foreign world.[23] Without delving into the debates regarding whether the New Testament is rightly considered a pre-millennial document or whether pre-millennialism is historically "new," I wish simply to observe that pre-millennialism is confronting its strongest opposition as the movement of Americanism permeates historically pre-millennial churches. To put it as strongly as possible, evangelical politics is *killing* pre-millennialism. The Americanist movement appears to be a mixture of influences in the American church's past: Puritan post-millennialism and the Constantinian desire for political significance or control.[24] It seems that the only thing keeping conservative evangelical Christians from totally abandoning the strong sense of hope typified by a "between the times" mentality is that they haven't won very many elections, at least not on the platform of being theologically conservative evangelicals. Should such a person finally win a presidential campaign (something rather unlikely given the, albeit unrealized, minority status of Christianity in the world, including, and perhaps especially, in the United States), Christians would readily expect that life on earth would begin to resemble the promised kingdom, if not even be the realization of it.[25] It is a very real question as to what hope would look like then.[26]

---

23. See e.g., Millard Erickson, *Christian Theology*, one volume edition (Grand Rapids: Baker, 1987) 1209–12.

24. "Manifest destiny" is perhaps the best illustration of how post-millennialism was translated into an official position espoused by the government. Conquest and settlement of the American frontier were natural outcomes of manifest destiny beliefs. God's people in God's new land laid the foundation for western expansionism in the new world.

25. This was clearly the mindset of the fundamentalism of the late 1800's and early 1900's. William Jennings Bryan ran for president several times on such a platform. He saw the opportunity to swell his support base amongst fundamentalist Christians by volunteering his services as prosecutor at the Scopes trial of 1925 in Tennessee. The famous outcome still reverberates throughout fundamentalist and evangelical circles, causing ongoing debate about the relationship of the Bible to culture. More to the point of our conversation, fundamentalists of that era, much like fundamentalists of today, seemed devastated by the loss of cultural influence to liberalism. Remarking on the drive of fundamentalism for cultural control, Carl F. H. Henry ("The Vigor of the New Evangelicalism," *Christian Life* [January, 1948] 32) observes, "Fundamentalism was not wrong in assuming a final consummation of history, but rather in assuming *this is it*."

26. Dobson is careful to attempt to remain pre-millennial by avoiding the social optimism propagated by post-millennialists. He is not convinced that the world will somehow get better if Christians are put in power. However, he doesn't see the inconsistency of his position: the attempt to restore the culture to traditional values has as its ultimate goal the betterment of society. According to pre-millennialism, such betterment can never

DOMESTICATED GLORY

Perhaps a clearer theological discussion could be had if the matter was situated in the context of God's sovereignty over all nations. Daniel affirms again and again the power of God to raise up kingdoms and place whomever He wishes in power (e.g., Dan 4:17, 25, 34–35). Daniel further makes it evident that the final Kingdom will be one that is established by the Son of Man—Jesus (7:14). Little disagreement exists over these passages. The apparent inconsistency arises when humans become determined to grant a specific earthly kingdom the divine status due only Christ's Kingdom. In other words, God's sovereignty seems unacknowledged in the kingdom of America. I am not referring to the way in which American Christians pay tribute to God's goodness over the many gracious opportunities granted by Him throughout the centuries. Indeed, tribute to God, though rarely Jesus, is a consistent theme in many national documents, slogans, and songs—e.g., "God Bless America!" Instead, I am referring to the way in which American Christians ignore the possibility that God's sovereignty may be expressed toward America in a fashion similar to the manner in which He has confronted all nations, including Israel: with judgment. What if America's greatest testimony to the sovereignty of God is her destruction and downfall? With such a fundamental relationship established between America and Christianity in current evangelical

---

occur this side of Christ's return. Things will continue to get worse. Pre-millennialism's only consolation is that perhaps because of societal degeneration the church will be purified and afforded a clearer witness. See James Dobson, "Family News From Dr. James Dobson" (June, 1999) 3; and James Dobson, "Family News From Dr. James Dobson" (August, 1999) 3.

An interesting parallel to evangelical social optimism can be made to the crisis that exists within many black churches today. As many black churches's message evolved into a message of emancipation and civil rights, the hope of the gospel was traded for a realization of individual rights and equality within a racially mixed society. The great tragedy, though certainly the abuse of bigotry and the horror of slavery was by all accounts a great tragedy as well, is that communities that once had the capacity to embody hope in a very real sense can hardly muster enough hope to imagine what Jesus's kingdom might look like. A grand illustration of this can be seen in the way that the Kingdom of America has plucked the voice of hope from within the black church that once spoke of Jesus's redemption and freedom and made him a symbol of the freedom for which all America stands. By making a national hero of Martin Luther King, Jr. and celebrating his cries for emancipation in a national holiday, America has silenced his hope in Jesus by reinterpreting him as a voice for all men everywhere, rallying around that universal good known as freedom. Hope, that is hope in Christ and His freedom, is dying in some black churches. Cf. Stanley Hauerwas, "Remembering Martin Luther King Remembering," *Wilderness Wanderings: Probing Twentieth Century Theology and Philosophy* (Boulder, CO: Westview, 1997) 225–37.

The Deceptive Allure of Home

politics, it is a real question whether the American church and its view of God's providence could survive the fall of America. Likely, American Christians have such confidence in the success of western political ideologies, they hardly think of God's sovereignty in such terms.

Another significant question to ask in this regard is "Whither Israel?" What is the future of Israel if America is a "Christian nation" established by God to be His chosen people? A familiar passage often quoted with patriotic enthusiasm in American churches is 2 Chronicles 7:14, "[If] My people who are called by My name humble themselves and pray, and seek My face and turn from their wicked ways, then I will hear from heaven, will forgive their sin, and will heal their land." I have stopped counting the number of times I've heard this passage quoted with regard to America as a nation. While I recognize that some principles of repentance from this passage may be quite applicable to the American church, the passage is usually used in such quotes with reference to the return of national America to its Christian roots.[27] Not having any passages in Scripture that mention America specifically, even pre-millennialists have now begun to apply to America passages directed toward the nation of Israel. The future of Israel as God's chosen nation is suspect when American Christians are laying such strong claim to their status as a Christian nation.

I suppose I could also have just as easily titled this chapter "Are we witnessing the death of missions?" since strong commitments to America tend to diminish missionary concerns. Indeed, Americanism kills missions, or at least distorts it to the extent that missions becomes a witness

---

27. I am not opposed to the notion that many of the founding fathers of the United States were most definitely committed Christians. The problem is with their doctrinal positions regarding the church and eschatology. With regard to the church, they generally succumbed to the attractiveness of individual autonomy and the rejection of authority; both of which are outstanding Revolutionary/Enlightenment doctrines, but not particularly Biblical doctrines. As a consequence of such heightened individualism, the church was, and still is, simply a collection of individuals, rather than a body that transcends the sum total of its parts. Eschatologically speaking, they were, for the most part, post-millennial, meaning they had a view of the United States as God's new heaven and new earth.

A second related problem centers on the notion that a commitment to Christianity by the founders somehow necessitates an infallibility of sorts when they turned their attention to nationalism. If such an assumption were made today—that everything Godly men do somehow translates into a plan blessed by God—we could conceivably have industries that are more Godly than others because they were founded by Christian businessmen, etc. We hardly recognize the inspired nature of Christian foundations in other matters; I fail to see the peculiar status of political ideologies.

to hoping in democracy, human rights, or some other Enlightenment ideology of freedom, rather than hoping in Christ. How many times have we prayed for the freedom of persecuted Christians, *rather than* praying for their faithful endurance, even unto death? Certainly, praying for freedom from persecution is not wrong, but we in the west tend to see it as the only real answer to persecution. If we no longer believe we live between the times, then evangelism becomes an effort to correct problems at a policy level in the political realm so that we can all live like the Christians we claim to be as citizens of "free nations."[28] Our regard for Paul's notion of our "citizenship in heaven" (Phil 3:20) becomes, at best, equivocal with a democratic ideology, and at worst, is simply forgotten or postponed.

Some outside observers seem to have confused evangelical politics with the building of an authoritarian "theocracy."[29] The fear of the left seems centered on the notion that Christians are not merely involved in politics; they wish to "take over" the entire political agenda in America, dismantling years of democracy in favor of establishing God's kingdom where God's people are the ones in charge. From the rhetoric and stated intentions of some proponents of evangelical politics, it may seem warranted to believe that Christians are working toward the transformation of America into a nation committed to the Law of Moses and an ethic

---

28. America boasts an incredible belief in God each time a poll is taken. However, it seems illegitimate to claim such a belief translates easily into Christian commitment. The optimistic notion that Christians are the majority in America, making American democracy a divine calling, seems to reach beyond Biblical parameters. Such notions can make elections interesting, giving them the flavor of spiritual warfare. The election of a favored candidate is a peaceful resolution to the conflict, allowing Christians to live in peace until the next election year. However, the temptation to control destiny through elections may in fact be Satan's way of compromising our commitment to God's way of ordering His authority, even as Satan was prone to tempt Jesus with power and control. Jesus's patience and dedication were unswerving and taught us the pursuit of the ultimate peace—peace with God (e.g., Matt 4:1–11; 26:36–46). We, like the disciples, seem attracted to the allure of power. Please don't misunderstand the point here. This does not mean we should not vote. I am simply drawing attention to our own overconfidence in the power of the election process.

29. A few good examples of such works include: Kevin Phillips, *American Theocracy: The Peril and Politics of Radical Religion, Oil, and Borrowed Money in the 21st Century*, (New York: Viking, 2006); James Rudin, *The Baptizing of America: The Religious Right's Plans for the Rest of Us* (New York: Thunder's Mouth, 2006); Michelle Goldberg, *Kingdom Coming: The Rise of Christian Nationalism* (New York: Norton, 2006); Randall Balmer, *Thy Kingdom Come: How the Religious Right Distorts the Faith and Threatens America: An Evangelical's Lament* (New York: Basic, 2006).

reflecting "born again" morality. Indeed, the chapters below are intended to demonstrate that evangelicals have committed themselves to strategies and ideologies that are political in nature and, by clear implication, unbiblical. However, the accusation that the religious right is purposefully attempting to overthrow democracy by establishing God's rule simply misses the point of evangelical politics. Robert Reich, former U.S. Labor Secretary under President Bill Clinton, displayed such misunderstanding several months prior to the 2004 presidential election.

> The great conflict of the 21st century may be between the West and terrorism. But terrorism is a tactic, not a belief. The underlying battle will be between modern civilization and anti-modernist fanatics; between those who believe in the primacy of the individual and those who believe that human beings owe blind allegiance to a higher authority; between those who give priority to life in this world and those who believe that human life is no more than preparation for an existence beyond life; between those who believe that truth is revealed solely through scripture and religious dogma, and those who rely primarily on science, reason, and logic. Terrorism will disrupt and destroy lives. But terrorism is not the only danger we face.

If one actually reads the substantive works, as well as the propaganda, it is very evident that the religious right in America is not committed to another form of government. Quite the contrary! They are in every way attempting to defend and restore what they believe is historical democracy. Far from propagating a conspiracy to subvert democracy, they rally in favor of the Enlightenment traditions undergirding democracy. Those who bemoan the "anti-modernist" fervor of the religious right fail to understand the ways in which modernism is being embraced and defended by evangelicals. The left seems unaware of the ways in which the religious right has become thoroughly modern in its philosophical and political commitments. In their defense, I would argue the right has come to these commitments somewhat blindly. But dismissing the religious right as William Jennings Bryan re-incarnate is simply naïve. Further, to accuse them of engaging in an attempt to conquer Western democracy is so much rhetoric.[30] As will be demonstrated below, it is actually the right's

---

30. Ross Douthat ("Theocracy, Theocracy, Theocracy," *First Things* 165 [August/September, 2006] 29–30) makes the salient point that the religious right's commitment to religion in politics is but a response to the left's secularist commitments of the early 1970s.

defense of democracy and autonomy of the individual that is domesticating the church.

CONCLUSION

While I am a pre-millennialist, I have no interest in defending the doctrine of pre-millennialism *per se* here. I believe it best represents the teaching of Scripture and seems to accord best with how each of the Biblical authors relates the church to the world. The Lordship of Jesus, as it is displayed in the church, is the means for proclaiming His supremacy to the world. A day will come when we will see His supremacy displayed over all the earth. We have briefly observed the disparity between the evangelical confidence in Americanism and Scripture's portrayal of Christianity's future hope. I am profoundly concerned about what the Americanist movement is doing to the Lordship of Christ within the church, though I must say the church was certainly ripe for its members to become disillusioned. The church in America is defined politically by its power in the polls (i.e., numbers), and Jesus has been reduced to a grand welfare provider for the emotionally and psychologically disabled from every social class. To discuss the political nature of the church and the power of Jesus's message no longer resonates in a world steeped in comfort and self-preservation. With such motifs as a backdrop, it is not difficult to see how placement of the Christian community in the world has been difficult. The church seems bent on becoming a better version of the world. However, before turning our attention more explicitly to the issue of the church in the world, it seems necessary to set the stage a bit further by illustrating some of the more popular sentiments of the "preservation of the Christian heritage" mindset. The politics of control over culture goes well beyond a few slogans and Bible verses. It is a business that plays on the fears of those whose hope in the Lord is easily shaken and whose perspective is challenged by constant awareness of the devastation in the world around us. Make no mistake; the world is not a pleasant place to live. It could, and likely will, get worse. I sympathize with those who are dismayed by the world and seek to protect themselves. However, I am not convinced our answer lies in building a better world, nor is it found in building a bigger wall between us and the world. Our answer, our hope, lies elsewhere— somewhere higher than earthbound eyes can see.

TWO

Finding Constantine

Evangelicals in the Politics of Postmodernism

THE HERITAGE OF THE Enlightenment stands as a somewhat ironic love/hate relationship for many evangelicals today. Two divergent strands in the heritage of Enlightenment thought have emerged. Consequently, two separate camps have developed that are diametrically opposed to one another. The first strand is an extreme indulgence into the autonomous individual. Postmodern deconstructionism has taught the world how to leverage any and every situation to one's own personal advantage. To deconstruct is to expose and, typically, to reject any instance of authority. Deconstructionists are primarily concerned with demonstrating the ways in which any appeal to authority can be made (e.g., foundationalism, rationalism, etc.). Such appeals can then be denied by rejecting the philosophical grounding for external authorities. Typically, this means denying the modern appeal to rational foundations for knowledge (thus, the term "*post*modern"). Deconstructionism only works in places where personal freedom reigns supreme. Its attraction is discovered precisely in the way it levels the playing field for everyone in the conversation. Politics, for deconstructionists, is no longer an appeal to a logical scheme best reflecting the workings of the world, nor is it an appeal to a system of ethics demonstrating the most benefit for the most people or at the least expense. Instead, politics suddenly becomes a matter of personal preference. The Enlightenment "turn to the subject" is completed in postmodernism with the subject now understanding itself as the supreme political power.[1] In other words, the autonomy of the individual is fully realized

---

1. In Enlightenment history, the "turn to the subject" refers to the way in which all reality came to be measured by the rational subject (i.e., individual human reason), rather than some external object or standard defining reality for the subject. What this

in that personal preference has become the ultimate political power. This is personal politics, despite "communal" rhetoric meant to build support for a position. Make no mistake; deconstructionism and democracy are clearly political allies. Deconstructionism is the full flower of democracy minus the benevolence of corporate concern for the welfare of a collective interest (e.g., the state). It should not surprise us that the politics of the self so prevalent in deconstructionism would find a home in democratic ideology. The self remains king in each model. This is the first strand of Enlightenment heritage.

The second strand of thought deriving from the Enlightenment is discovered in the reaction of conservatives against deconstructionist pluralism. Evangelicals are finding it more and more difficult to function in a postmodern world so devoted to the preservation of the self. In a reactionary move, many evangelicals have trumpeted the political right to religious preference. However, the individual liberty that seemed like a promising political avenue to pursue now represents a suicidal move theologically. Many still see promise in the retreat to individual religious liberties—that the best way to protect and promote religious belief is to represent it as a moment of personal reflection comparable to any other personal belief, in other words, an individual right. Of course, the difficulty of such a position is that it reduces the Lordship of Jesus to *mere* personal belief. It becomes one more of the many political players on the level of personal politics—a simple matter of private preference. In other words, for all practical purposes, promoting individual religious liberties simply affirms pluralism. Evangelicals who wish to make bold universal pronouncements about their belief in the Lordship of Jesus are either dismissed by deconstructionists as another group appealing to rhetoric beyond the scope of personal politics or they are confronted as unwilling to play by the rules of full blown democracy (i.e., pluralism). Any appeal to individual religious liberties or rights simply places evangelicals into a position of limited power, which of course is a primary goal of deconstructionism. Gone are the days of Constantinian presumption where the

---

meant for theology is that even the existence of God was submitted to the scrutiny of human reason in order to determine if He could be regarded as real (cf. René Descartes, *Meditations on First Philosophy*, trans. by Donald Cress [Indianapolis: Hackett, 1993] paragraphs 1-2). Revelation, as seen in the Biblical text, did not fare well under the eye of the rational subject, since revelation records several events unacceptable to human reason. Unfortunately, many models of Christian apologetics today still pander to the autonomy of human reason by appealing to reason as the ultimate authority.

state and church could be seen as ultimate expressions of human reality and destiny. We now live in a (postmodern) world of personal ultimates where individual expressions of destiny are the status quo—i.e., relativism. The difficulty for evangelicals is discovered in the question, "How do Christians avoid reducing their universal claims to mere individual preferences?"

In contrast to the postmodern claim of power in the individual, evangelicals, along another vein, have asserted the historical priority of universal absolutes based in an external source or authority. These universal absolutes are the product of well-thought principles of human rationality available and demonstrable to any rational creature. This is more purely a defense of Enlightenment rationality based in the egalitarianism of individual reason. Here, the neo-modernist search for absolutes leads against relativism, but unfortunately, also leads away from the more secure foundation of revelation. Of course, in the world of politics and power, *numbers* are convincing. In order to appeal to the largest number of rational minds and secure the greatest level of support, evangelicals have translated, that is *reduced*, the language of Scripture to principles or universal statements of value that will appeal to a broader audience. For the purpose of attracting more people to the life prescribed by Scripture—a life conforming to Judeo-Christian values—evangelicals have created a universal language derived from the principles of Scripture.[2] This translation of revelation into universal language can often be seen in the moral code of "family values" or "traditional values." While certainly well intentioned, such a reduction of Scripture misses the point of revelation. Evangelicals now seem to resemble their liberal foes of decades ago (e.g., Bultmann) who taught that the real meaning of Scripture is discovered in the hidden meaning beneath the text. In the process of discovering how to make Scripture appeal to the broader audience (the politics of numbers), evangelicals have emasculated the power of the language in which God chose to express Himself and the community that is His witness. In our attempt to make Scripture more understandable or memorable, conforming or translating it to the language of moral principles, we have in fact transformed Christianity into a moral code or religion appealing to the politics of the conservative masses (e.g., "family values" or "traditional

---

2. E.g., see Carole G. Adams, "Biblical-Classical: The Principle Approach Model of Education," *The Foundation for American Christian Education Newsletter* 12 (April, 2005).

values"). Let me make this plain; evangelicals have, in many instances, become convinced that a more secure foundation exists than revelation. Enlightenment rationality has enticed evangelicals to grant authority to principles, or universal absolutes, that, while they are purported to be derived from Scripture, are in fact a human creation lifted to the same plane as God's revealed word. The reliability of human rationality has replaced trust in divine revelation.

Of course, one might argue that all Christian preaching is the result of deriving principles from the text of revelation. I am certainly aware that we are constantly in need of explanation and help in understanding Scripture. The difference between preaching and the discussion of principles discovered as explanations of revelation is that preaching remains connected to the Scripture as something intended to assist in understanding. In contrast, the principles of "traditional values" in contemporary politics are intended to stand on their own as representative of a moral code agreeable to all cultures adhering to a Judeo-Christian heritage. In other words, since it is impossible to write Scripture into legislation, the principles must be a code unto themselves, i.e., self-referential.

In light of such a strong trust in principles that are purported to have been derived from Scripture, but in actuality stand alone, the deconstructionist critique of Enlightenment rationality may actually provide a great service to the church. The attention drawn by deconstructionists to the problems associated with vesting authority in Enlightenment rationality serve as a good reminder that no foundation exists that is more secure than revelation. Of course, many deconstructionists would hardly agree that their critique of the Enlightenment should lead to such a conclusion. Nevertheless, their critique rightly points us to the only sure source of knowledge: God's self-revelation as seen in His Word.

IS THE CHURCH REALLY MORE IMPORTANT THAN THE FAMILY?

I make no bones about the fact that I like Dr. James Dobson. I find I admire his, and at times even the late Jerry Falwell's, unabashed Christian testimony in the public square. On most occasions where he addresses social issues, Dobson attempts to promote a Christian testimony first and foremost. Further, one of the greatest achievements accomplished by those who wish for evangelicals to take political activity more seriously is the way in which they have countered the inherent Gnostic tendencies in evangelicalism, driven as it is by its understanding of conversion as hope in a life after death. With evangelicalism's focus centered on converting the soul in order to secure a person's eternal destiny for Christ, we have seen little focus on living the material life given to us by God on this earth that endures for years, even decades, after conversion. A theology of life in the human body is woefully lacking amongst evangelicals today. Politics and those appealing to evangelical involvement have thankfully drawn attention to the needed consideration of how to live the human life as a testimony to a lost and dying world.

Unfortunately, the attempts by evangelicals to insert themselves into the political process are occasionally fraught with inconsistencies and misunderstandings that make the relationship of the church to the world rather unclear. On other occasions, evangelicals have had a tendency to act more like politicians or power brokers for a political movement than as theologians for the church.[3] For example, while it is readily apparent that Dobson's familial advice can be quite helpful to family life, as long as he relies on Scripture rather than the secular anthropology of psychology, he has unwittingly contributed to the belief that family is somehow an

---

3. Like Carl Henry and Russell Moore in the previous chapter, Dobson seems to have succumbed to the false dichotomy that only two positions exist. Either the church is a major player in the political arena or it is isolationistic. Such a narrowing of the options has blinded them to the possibility of having a political witness along lines other than the politics of the world. For Dobson, and others who wish to shape culture, the power of the church is finally found in voting booths and lobbying efforts. Though some may wish to argue that those evangelicals attempting to shape culture through politics are merely working on the moral life of the church and are not engaging in the arenas of worship or evangelism (i.e., the internals of the church), they don't realize that such a segregation/fragmentation of the church is part of the problem. The moral life of the church is as much its worship and evangelism as anything else it says or does. The church cannot, indeed, it must not, reduce its message of life in Christ to a few intellectual statements or a list of "family values." Of course, it would be unfair to lay all this at the doorstep of Dobson and his ministry. Others are just as guilty, if not more so. However, he seems to illustrate well the, albeit unintentional, separation of the moral life of the church from the Gospel. See Dobson, "Family News From Dr. James Dobson," (June, 1999) 1–3. Dobson attempts to place his debate in the context of securing "traditional values," but his war is in reality a struggle for control or power over who sets the rules and agenda for life in America (2). Of course, this reduces the church to merely another political voice. As John MacArthur ("The Deadly Danger of Moralism," *The Master's Seminary Mantle* 9 [2002] 4) points out, "When the church elevates the pursuit of cultural morality above the biblical mandate to proclaim the gospel, it essentially forfeits its distinctive voice and takes its place among a myriad of lobbyist groups and political parties peddling earthly agendas."

institution on a par with the church. I say unwittingly because I believe he has good intentions to help families as a part of the church. However, in recent years, Focus on the Family has stated as one of its guiding principles that "God has ordained three basic institutions—the church, the family and the government—for the benefit of all humankind."[4] John MacArthur makes a similar claim when he states

> 4. Such a notion pervades much of the literature calling for American Christians to get involved in their government. This citation of Focus on the Family's guiding principle was reiterated in conjunction with Tom Minnery, "The Relationship between Church, Family and Government," *Focus on the Family* (July, 1998) 10-12. Minnery is the vice president of Public Policy at Focus on the Family.
>
> I cannot help but note the anthropocentrism of Focus on the Family's principle, the words "for the benefit" of society, or "all humankind," being the operative terms. At one level I think this is right that the church does exist as a witness to all humankind, which is obviously for its benefit. But the benefit of humanity is hardly the purpose of the church, or the Gospel, or any institution created by God. Indeed, for such to be the case is for God to place something above His own desire to glorify Himself and bring honor to His name first and foremost. If left at the mere level of its benefit to humanity, the Gospel amounts to an idolatrous obsession with humanity.
>
> Ultimately, what Minnery's statement seems directed toward is making society a place in which being a Christian is a safe or good thing to be. Christianity naturally becomes, in this scenario, a set of principles by which to live a better life. But if Jesus was merely trying to turn people toward living a better life, why kill Him? If Jesus was simply trying to make the culture a place that would better the lives of all humans who participate in it, why try to silence Him? Wouldn't any culture, Jewish, Roman, or otherwise, want this for itself?
>
> Indeed it is a perplexing, and perhaps somewhat convicting, question to ask why the Jews were finally upset with Jesus. After praising Him as the coming Messiah only a few days before, they suddenly turned and called for His crucifixion. Obviously, as Scripture states, the Jewish leaders were behind much of this turnabout (Matt 27:20). But from a more purely political perspective, it's difficult for us to grasp this change. We, perhaps like some of Jesus's early followers, have come to believe that Jesus was merely outlining a way to be a better people, i.e., to live according to moral principles, to be more psychologically stable, to have better families and marriages, to handle our money more frugally, etc. Jesus doesn't seem very dangerous in this context. He was merely trying to help us better ourselves. He was offering teachings that could give us more opportunity (as if Jesus's mission is so simplistically explained in anthropocentric terms). Thus, it baffles us that anyone would wish to kill such a kindly man who was only looking out for our welfare.
>
> On the contrary, it appears the only plausible way to explain Jesus's murder is as a result of Jewish and Roman nationalism. In different ways, Jesus was an affront to the patriotic sentiments of both the Jews and the Romans. The problem was that He was not enough of a Messiah for the Jews and He was too much of one for the Romans. When Jesus was crucified as the "King of the Jews," this was a statement about how the kingdoms of this world did and would react to His claims of Lordship. We do an injustice to the significance of His death if we understand it solely as a result of theological differences between Jesus and the Jewish leaders over the Law. Interestingly, the Jewish leaders and the Romans may have been the only ones who really grasped the political extent of

> Nowhere should the social aspect of the new man be more evident than in the home, the single most important social institution in the world . . . It is difficult to see how Christianity can have any positive effect on society if it cannot transform its own homes.[5]

It has become such a commonplace belief that the family is a more primary moral institution than the church that it sounds like heresy to challenge such a presumption. But of course, that is exactly what Jesus did when he delineated the cost of following after Him, of being a part of His church (Luke 14:25–35), and when He asked who were His mother and brother and sister (Matt 12:46–50). Jesus goes so far as to say that He "did not come to bring peace, but a sword. For I came to set a man against his father, and a daughter against her mother . . ." (Matt 10:34ff.). This sword is not a sword of violence or hatred between believers and their families. Instead, it is a sword of separation. If forced to choose which is more important, Jesus makes it clear that being His follower, a member of His body, is pre-eminent. Likewise, Paul even finds the single life more in line with the life to which God has called those who would serve Him

---

Jesus's claims. They understood, rightly, that Jesus was/is a threat to all authorities in this world.

One could even read the hostility of the Jews against the Gentiles who were entering the church in Acts as a result of lingering Jewish nationalism, rather than simply a religious issue regarding the Law. Indeed, perhaps the Law is better understood in such a context as a national symbol, much like a flag or document of national constitution, instead of a religious qualifier. It seems not so much the substance of the Law that was at issue, though that was certainly the way it was presented, as it was allegiance to the Jewish way of being one of God's chosen. The church was a challenge to what it meant to be a Jew in the first century. No wonder some of the Jews were actively seeking to kill Christians (e.g., Saul).

In an analogous way, Americanism is crucifying the Lordship of Christ all over again by translating the political nature of His universal claims into a temporal political ideology. Thus, we modern Christians find it acceptable, even exemplary, to be committed to both Christ and nation. The primary virtue in such a setting then becomes balance. One needs to balance the demands of nation with the claims of Christ and find a way to be committed to one without compromising the commitment to the other. Of course, what this means is that, at times, one must re-read the claims of one (most often Christ) in light of the other (nation). Consequently, the claims of one (Christ) are *made compatible with* (reduced to? translated into?) the claims of the other (nation). One can easily see how balance ultimately becomes the virtue of mediocrity. As mentioned above, such reduction of Christ's claims for the sake of compatibility, or common ground, is a major step on the path toward liberalism.

5. John MacArthur, *Colossians and Philemon*, MacArthur Bible Studies (Nashville: Thomas Nelson, 2007) 71–72.

unreservedly (1 Cor 7:8, 25–35). Make no mistake, Paul is certainly not saying it is a sin to marry and have a family—I have one myself and love them dearly. Scripture has much to say about marriage and family, making it an important aspect of life in Christ. I do not wish to demean family or marriage by pointing out Biblical priorities. Family is important; I am simply pointing to the Biblical fact that it is not primary.

Unfortunately, many today often tend to think of Jesus as though He were representative of the "ultimate family man" or the "epitome of family values"—the perfect husband and father, metaphorically speaking, of course. (Compare this to the likewise ahistorical conception of Jesus as the "superhuman" by the liberal theologians of Nazi Germany—Jesus became a "set of principles" for them too.) We forget that Jesus never married or had any children. The primary social institution He wished to promote was His church. That is where morality and discipline were to be learned first and foremost.[6] Certainly, He hadn't forgotten the commands to be fruitful or to honor father and mother. But He brought a different mindset with Him when He appeared on the earth. He came to shatter idols considered sacred by the Jews of His day, one of those idols being the family (Matt 10:34–39). We are prone today to see singleness as less than God's intentions for us as Christians, or even for us as humans. Jesus and Paul seem to place the burden of proof on the other foot. Instead of asking single men and women to justify their singleness, Jesus and Paul seem to ask married people for their justification to be married. In light of the encompassing claims of the gospel and the inherent distractions of marriage, this may prove somewhat difficult for us.

---

6. It is interesting to note the odd mixture of political philosophies in conservative politics today. The call often goes out for men and women who are of substantive character to fill the roles of political office, while battles rage on the level of principles and issues. Though other sources may be cited, this is in many respects a mixture of Aristotle, who believed character was at issue in becoming a virtuous person, and Plato, who searched for a principle(s) on which to base his moral reasoning on various issues. The danger I find is when people are drawn toward establishing principles (universal moral absolutes or traditional values) as the primary moral reference for the Christian community. If you obey the letter of the law, you may then be considered virtuous or righteous. We have become adept at creating modern Pharisees and our own "traditions of men" that we add to the Gospel. However, as is made clear in a Biblical discussion of ecclesiology, being church involves being apprenticed/discipled into the moral life. Plato's, and Immanuel Kant's, approach to the moral life amounts to a form of liberal politics in the way they expect the principle, or law, to effect moral change.

Finding Constantine

Many in today's society are working hard to rebuild this idol. The family has become a more powerful institution in our Christian world than the church. As Tom Minnery indicates, "Society has yet to invent a better means of raising healthy, well-adjusted people than by placing them in loving and intact families that live under godly principles."[7] While it must be granted that "society" has definitely not invented anything better than the family, God most certainly has. The church was Jesus's and the apostles's primary moral institution. This obviously does not mean that the family is unimportant, but if forced to choose between the two, Jesus leaves little room for discussion. God and His family come first.[8]

---

7. Minnery, "Relationship between Church, Family and Government," 10. What Minnery fails to realize is that society is working hard to challenge God's pattern of what a Christian community in the world should look like precisely as it develops the notion of "family values" or "traditional values." Establishing "family values" appears to be an attempt to reduce Christianity to a set of principles that could be advocated by any "reasonable" conservative. I suspect that both Constantine and Kant would be proud to find they had convinced Christians to arrive at such a notion. Jesus, on the other hand, seems conspicuously absent from such a scheme, other than perhaps to provide us with an example of how to live up to those principles (à la the social gospel?).

Interestingly, Jesus probably wouldn't survive in the world of "family values." After all, He remained single and seemed to regard those who followed after Him, who were His responsibility (John 17:6–12), as more important than His biological relatives. (Even His concern for His mother while He was hanging on the cross [John 19:26–27] proves the point of Christian community as prior to family—that He could expect the apostle John would care for an old widow(?) who was not biologically in his sphere of concern.)

Perhaps a better way to enter this discussion is to ask the question, "Who owns our children?" I think perhaps Minnery's statement demonstrates he rightly understands such a question. Unfortunately, he answers it according to the world's terms. It is a fact that the state claims to own our children; and it is happy to exercise such ownership if it feels we are not doing an appropriate job as parents. Minnery's claim implies that families own the children and have the right to be the first and perhaps only influence in their lives. While I am not an advocate of infant baptism, I recognize that it served for centuries to remind us all that children are first and last owned by God. The purpose of raising them is not to make them "healthy, well-adjusted people," as Minnery claims. The purpose is to mold them into images of Christ, albeit small ones in small worlds. Minnery seems to have bought into the world's notion that children are to be valued for their "potential," rather than as a reflection of Godly faith toward which we are all to aim (Mark 10:13–16; Matt 18:1–6).

8. Dobson seems to believe this himself, since he is unwilling to leave families to their natural course. He knows that, if left without direction and guidance, families, like any sin laden institution, will deteriorate into social groups marked by power struggles and coercion, rather than love and self-sacrifice.

The inconsistency that becomes apparent in Dobson's work is that he wishes to correct family behavior while at the same time extolling the family as the primary moral institu-

It sounds almost heretical today to imagine that Jesus could have such a strong claim on our lives. We have been told by the Kingdom of America that we are free to do what we want—that we are all created equal and that we are free to determine our own destiny (i.e., the right to life, liberty, and the pursuit of happiness). God is supposed to be something that is only a private matter. How dare He make claims that could infringe on our rights to individual liberty! It is at this point that God has overstepped His bounds. Is it any wonder that Americans are prone to think of God as merely one option among the many over which the individual holds dominion?

Such sarcasm is meant simply to point out that American Christians have been seduced into believing the U.S. Constitution is somehow an inspired document that holds as much truth as, or perhaps even more truth than, Scripture. George Washington, James Madison, Thomas Jefferson, and other "Founding Fathers" have been given something that seems akin to apostolic authority. The Bill of Rights's and Declaration of Independence's claims to individual liberty are often regarded by evangelicals as though they have authority comparable to that of Scripture, perhaps even more so in this arena, since Scripture never discusses individual rights or liberties.[9] Certainly, Scripture tells us we have been freed from sin, but this freedom is not the removal of all constraints, as Enlightenment rationality would have it.[10] Instead, it is freedom to become enslaved to another master, to

---

tion. The question that makes this inconsistency clearer is "From where does Dobson get his authority? Is it from a family or from a group of believers not biologically related to him to whom he feels accountable?" I suspect Dobson would answer the latter, making it apparent that he implicitly believes the church takes primacy over the family. In other words, a level of accountability exists for which the church is responsible that extends well beyond any biological relationship (Matt 18:15–20).

9. The argument regarding Christian founders of the United States necessitating its qualification as a Christian nation is dubious at best. While I make no bones about the fact that some founders were Christians, this is hardly reason enough to grant infallibility to their ideology any more than we should grant such a status to a football team being a Christian team because they are all Christians and pray before a game or to a business being Christian because the owners profess a devout faith in Christ. In other words, faith does not necessarily equivocate with political ideology. History is replete with kings and queens who claimed Jesus as their own, and in fact, kings are discussed in the Bible. Does this make monarchian government the ideal form of government? Americans would roundly agree it does not. Yet, we are slow to recognize the way in which we have invested a democratic ideology with infallibility.

10. See Immanuel Kant, "What is Enlightenment?" in *Foundations of the Metaphysics of Morals*, ed. by Lewis White Beck (New York: Macmillan, 1959) 85–92.

gain bondage to righteousness, even God Himself (Rom 6:15–23). We are never told in Scripture that our life is our own to do with as we please. Paul recognizes no neutral (i.e., objective) standpoint from which we may determine our own course. We are either slaves to sin or slaves to God. We are not saved so that we may now become kings of our own destiny. The whole point of the New Covenant reality inaugurated by Christ is so that we might "walk in *His* statutes and be careful to observe *His* ordinances" (Ezek 36:27). "Like ancient Israel, the church is called to be a kingdom of priests, not a kingdom of social activists."[11]

Indeed, it is the height of arrogance to believe that God saved us primarily for *our* benefit (Ezek 36:22-32). We are consistently given the message in Scripture that "It is *He* who has made us, and not we ourselves; we are *His* people and the sheep of *His* pasture" (Ps 100:3). The Kingdom of God is one in which He reigns supreme, in which He has authority over those who call Him Lord. The Kingdom of America is one in which individuals believe they have the right to govern themselves because of the autonomy granted them by the Constitution, and even more, by their existence as enlightened individuals.[12] To submit to God is to surrender to the "laziness and cowardice" that caused humans to capitulate to their "self-incurred tutelage" or religious superstition for centuries.[13] To be subject to another is *not* to be truly free.[14] That is why, in the Kingdom of

11. John MacArthur, *Romans 9–16*, MacArthur New Testament Commentary (Chicago: Moody, 1994) 209.

12. Indeed, one of the indications of how deeply this belief of individual autonomy permeates our society is the debate over the separation of Christ's Lordship from His role as Savior. American Christians want the benefits of salvation without the encumbrance of submitting to another authority other than themselves. Little do they recognize that Christ is Lord over those who call Him Lord *and* over those who don't. In other words, He is Lord whether we like it or not. The difference is simply that some have come to realize it in this life. It will be a much happier day at His appearing for those who know He is Lord. It is the task of Christians to live a life that witnesses the reality of the Lordship of Christ, so that the world may see and find conversion (Phil 2:1–16). Living the Lordship of Jesus is how the church exists as church and how it makes the world know that it is the world. How quickly evangelicals have joined the liberals in forgetting that our God is the Lord of all creation. In other words, and I think I learned this from Stanley Hauerwas, the difference between the church and the world is the church knows who its king is; the world does not, at least, not yet.

13. This is, of course, Kant's description of what it means to be unenlightened. See Kant, "What is Enlightenment?" 85.

14. American Christians still operate under the presumption that true freedom is the removal of all constraints, with the only limits being non-infringement on an-

America, church and God must be only a part of our lives, alongside family and government, and not dominate our whole being. We must finally be lords of our lives, maintaining final control and authority over every aspect. Ultimately, freedom has become our god, and the "church must be bold if freedom is to flourish."[15] In such a context, it is an interesting question to ask, "What will happen to the church if/when America, or any other such post-Enlightenment experiment in democracy, fails?" Will we, like Daniel, live as God's people no matter what flag is flying, or will we go down with the stars and stripes?[16]

MAN AS THE HUB OF THEOLOGY

To put the question in more theological terms, perhaps we could ask, "What has happened to the Gospel today?" It seems that, at least since the Enlightenment, we have seen a shift toward a man-centered Gospel. Instead of viewing humans as a *means* to God's glory, our emphasis has evolved toward an anthropocentric Gospel in which human welfare becomes the primary *end* of the cross. This is not to say that such an emphasis is unique to modernity, but it does seem apparent that we have raised up a generation of Christian theology in which the central doctrine is anthropology. Many evangelicals are in the process of revising doctrines in light of this preference. What is meant by this is, put quite

---

other's rights. This is how people typically interpret the Declaration of Independence. Unfortunately, the apostle Paul has no such conception of freedom. Freedom from sin is not the removal of all constraints. Rather, it is enslavement to a new master—God (Rom 6:18, 22). Our truest fulfillment of God's intentions for humanity is found in unreserved devotion to Him, not in some notion of autonomy where God is brought down to our level and made a "partner" in the Christian life.

15. Minnery, "The Relationship between Church, Family and Government," 11. This is the flip side to Minnery's comment that "freedom must exist if the church is to flourish" (10). It is interesting to see how much freedom dominates his definition of what it means to be a part of the church. It seems for him, just as we cannot be Americans without freedom, likewise, it is difficult to be a Christian without being a self-determined American.

16. In many respects, the church today is in a situation similar to Daniel's. Just as he and his people were a community of believers without a nation, so too is the church that lives between the times. We are between the Israel of the Old Testament and the millennial kingdom; that's what it means to be pre-millennial. The church is a people without a land or country. As a consequence, we need to learn how to survive in a world that desires our allegiance and is willing to punish us if we don't bend the knee when it blows its horns. We have become so subtly coerced that we hardly recognize our allegiance to America as competing with our allegiance to God (Jas 4:4).

simply, meaning in theology is measured by first asking the question of human relevancy; indeed, any object that is external to the human subject has meaning only as it is perceived within the purview of human interpretation (e.g., Kant's categories). In such a scenario, Christianity, like all other religions, becomes merely a means for the improvement of human history. Human benefit is the final measure of religion's meaningfulness. Even psychologists recognize human benefit as the primary promise of religion.

> [The purpose of religion is to] impose equally on everyone its own path to the acquisition of happiness, and protection from suffering. Its technique consists in depressing the value of life and distorting the picture of the real world in a delusional manner—which presupposes an intimidation of the intelligence. At this price, by forcibly fixing them in a state of psychical infantilism and by drawing them into a mass-delusion, religion succeeds in sparing many people an individual neurosis. But hardly anything more. There are, as we have said, many paths which may lead to such happiness as is attainable by men, but there is none which does so for certain. Even religion cannot keep its promise.[17]

Freud's understanding of the value of religion, limited as he believes it is, is clearly anthropocentric. The similarity between the liberal vein of theology flowing from the "turn to the subject" and evangelicalism's transformation of the Gospel into what benefits humanity should be clear. The evangelical commitment to anthropology undermines Scriptural doctrines, such as God's sovereignty or supremacy over all things, to the extent that the Gospel is understood and presented in terms beneficial to human existence. This is not to say that the Gospel does not affect human circumstance; however, many evangelicals have made the change in circumstance the final message of the Gospel; it has become just another version of the Social Gospel. "Much like liberal Christians at the turn of the century, many evangelicals have lost their focus on eternal values and become enamored of temporal issues, creating what amounts to a politically conservative version of social Christianity."[18] Evangelical politics appears to be moving precisely in this direction as it connects theological confidence in humanity with the success of circumstance. Even if church and government remain disconnected, as they are for some, the theology

---

17. Sigmund Freud, *Civilization and Its Discontents* (New York: Norton, 1961) 36.
18. MacArthur, *Romans 9–16*, 208.

of American politics still seems to parallel the Gospel in that both exist for the welfare of human existence.

It is a fairly common belief today, amongst even the most devout evangelicals and fundamentalists, that "the family, church and government occupy separate spheres of life."[19] We believe we are part of a society in which we must constantly be weighing and balancing competing interests, all of which are legitimate.[20] Even as Christians, we have been taught

---

19. Minnery, "Relationship between Church, Family and Government," 12.

20. It seems a better way of putting the problem is as a problem of competing lords, rather than competing self-interests. God is not merely an interest of ours, He is Lord of the creation, of which we are a part. Unfortunately, we don't really believe any longer that God is the Lord of all that is. What we fail to realize is that these other competing interests also wish to be lords over us. We have become so bewitched by their allure and our capacity to be gods ourselves that we fail to see the powers as powers—the angel of light can look very bright. In other words, I am claiming that Christ's Lordship is entirely comprehensive and cannot be balanced against other interests. All other claims on the life of the believer, including our own claim to autonomy, are finally subsumed in our identity as Christians.

I wish to push this point a bit by asking again, by way of reminder, the question, "Who owns our children?" As mentioned above, we would almost instinctively respond "Why, the parents, of course!" But after pondering the question for a bit, we realize that the state actually claims to own our children. For if the state does not like the way we are raising our children or believes that we are somehow doing them harm in the way we raise them, then it will take them away and ask someone else to raise them in a manner the state approves. To push this even further, ask yourself the question, "Who owns me?" We would like to say God does, but again we remember that the state at times makes claims indicating that it wishes to exercise ownership. One such instance is the military draft, in which the state asks young men (and women?) to give their very lives for the sake of the preservation of the state and all of its incumbent privileges. Don't misunderstand my point here. Obviously, I am not trying to argue for becoming a tax-dodging rebel who wars against the state. Indeed, though I have seen and heard defenses of violence against oppressors, I am yet to be convinced that such revolutionary violence is justifiable on scriptural grounds. We are still to render unto Caesar what is Caesar's (Matt 22:15–22), including taxes, labor, respect, etc (Rom 13:7). Americans are finally forced to admit that this country originated from principles that are unbiblical, or as John MacArthur (*Romans 9–16*, 207) more forcefully puts it, "the United States was born out of violation of Scripture."

Of course, when Caesar asks us to render to him what is rightly due God, then we need to be prepared to suffer the consequences of following after our rightful Lord. Jesus never appears to be asking us to overthrow the state or worldly powers, by neither peaceful nor violent means. Submission seems to be the context of the New Testament church and the early church up to Constantine. I remain a bit baffled at our tremendous fear of martyrdom by the hands of the state after reading accounts of the early Christians. Death should not be a problem for those who really believe in Jesus, yet it is. Indeed, in the between times of the church, we have few other options. (For example, see how others who were under the regime of the world responded when faced with following either the only

Finding Constantine

(i.e., discipled by the world to believe) that we have a stake in seeing each institution, church, family, and government, succeed. Or perhaps I should say we are "being taught" that such is the case. For some believe that "For much of this century, the conservative Bible-believing church has turned its face from government, seeking to be separate rather than to be salt and light."[21] The consequence, of course, is that "society has suffered as a result."[22] The question that seems begging to be asked is "When did the church decide it had a stake in seeing society succeed?" In other words, "When did we decide that America is God's chosen nation and that this culture and political ideology is the one God wants to preserve (i.e., post-millennialism)?"

Perhaps such an attitude is more reflective of Constantinianism than it is of post-millennialism. Constantinianism is the wedding of Christianity to civil government that took place in 312 AD when Constantine became a Christian and declared Christianity to be an acceptable religion of the

---

true God or the world: Daniel 3, the martyrdom of most of the apostles, the martyrdom of many in the early church.) Could it be that we would really rather have our place in the world than be at home with the Lord?

If one doubts that the state seeks to be a lord over us, just imagine the Pledge of Allegiance to the American Flag as a prayer the next time you say it. I was initially surprised how much it sounds like a prayer of devotion to a master. Likewise, if one doubts the way in which people, particularly Christians, have devoted themselves to the god of America, try removing the pledge from the practices of a school, or simply stand at attention (Christians are still to show respect—Rom 13:7) silently while it is being said and watch for the dirty looks you'll be given. Or if you wish to be physically accosted, propose removing the American flag (and while you're at it, the Christian flag) from the front of the church. Would we ask foreign missionaries from America to pledge their allegiance to the flag of the country to which we send them?

Perhaps a more profound reason for our devotion to the Kingdom of America is that it is the only thing we moderns believe is worth dying for. We will gladly send our children to die for the country to refrains of "Over There," but we have profound reservations about dying for the church. I suspect we hardly even know what it means to die for the church, for Christ's body—for the faith, since we don't see it very often any more, at least not in America. Dying for freedom appears to be the predominant paradigm in virtue.

To his credit, Dobson has done the church a great service in this arena. His continued proclamation of the reality of martyrdom helps Christians in America know that the church is still alive out there somewhere. As long as Christians are still willing to die for their faith, there is hope that the church will not succumb to the belief that self-preservation and this life we have now are ends in themselves.

21. Minnery, "Relationship between Church, Family and Government," 12.
22. Ibid.

Roman world (313 AD—the Edict of Milan).[23] By the end of the century, Christianity was *the* official religion of the Roman world. Suddenly, Christianity had power and status in the political realm. It had a place in the world, and it was not afraid to use it. Some today seem to reminisce of those days, albeit perhaps implicitly, by placing their Christian hope in the powers the church could have in this world, or better, did have in this world when America was a Christian nation.[24] But what this longing for power fails to realize is a more plausible interpretation of the Constantine event may exist. Rather than being a moment of triumph for the church, it was instead a moment in which the church was coerced into giving up the power it had through the Gospel. Constantine saw that Christians were becoming a powerful witness precisely because of their unwillingness to recant their faith and, likewise, because of their willingness to submit to the state finally in martyrdom. Such commitment evinced an authentic witness of the Christian belief that death is not the final enemy and that Jesus is Lord not only over the state, but even over death itself. By claiming that the church cannot witness to the world unless it is involved in trying to make the world better, Minnery appears to dismiss the notion that death is perhaps a stronger witness than life. Death, in the context of the evangelical desire to create a Christian nation, becomes politically meaningless. The greater virtue is death for king and country. Perhaps this is why Jesus's death has such an uninfluential place in politics. Instead of being a real Jew who died on the cross, Jesus must be a set of principles upon which to build a Christian society. His teachings have become more important than His person, since Jesus is now a mere resource to improve the human condition. In such a political context as this, coercion by

---

23. Of course, Constantine retained certain powers, such as the right to act as the official leader of the newly accepted religion. In this, he was merely exercising the same sovereignty over religion all previous Roman leaders had assumed. We see this right of sovereignty being exercised most clearly in 321 when Constantine called and presided over the council at Nicea.

24. A parallel exists here between our conception of power and the perceived power of the Jews in the Old Testament. A temptation that existed for them and their leaders, especially David, was to place their confidence in numbers, or their capacity for strength in battle. However, God regards David's numbering of his warriors and armaments as a sin (e.g., 1 Chr 21). Likewise, even the numbering in the book of Numbers is not intended to show how strong Israel is in the face of her enemies. Instead, God is attempting to demonstrate His own strength and glory as He fulfills His promises to the people of Israel for a land, a nation, and a blessing (Gen 12:1–3). See Ronald B. Allen, *Numbers*, Expositor's Bible Commentary 2 (Grand Rapids: Zondervan, 1990) 690–91.

Finding Constantine

profound principles becomes the tool of change, rather than witness and conversion. Coercion is the *world's* tool it wields each time it lobbies in political halls and preaches the power of collective bodies in a democracy. Most politicians, Christians included, are quite adept at the art of coercion, but in the midst of this, witness is being redefined or even sacrificed for the sake of something called the "common good."[25]

> 25. This seems to be the best place to offer some explanation for my heightened ecclesiology. I have no doubt that many will feel I am unnecessarily offending people by drawing such stark contrasts between the church and the world, and by construing many who are trying to serve the church as, instead, servants of the world. My only response is that a strong emphasis on the Lordship of Christ over His church and the fact that the church is the institution through which He has chosen to demonstrate that Lordship seems warranted given Christ's own concern for the church. Some may find this offensive, but such offense may be the result of being lulled into committing ourselves to other gods in the world, albeit implicitly.
>
> Others may wish to defend Enlightenment principles of autonomy and rationality in their exuberance to make America the greatest nation that has ever existed or ever will exist (read again post-millennialism here, since it seems unreasonable to some in this camp that God could invent anything better than various forms of democracy). However, they need to understand exactly what it is they are defending. The individualism wrought by Enlightenment thinkers, including the founders of our own republic, advocates independence from not only the community we call church, but even from God Himself. The notion that we are rights-bearing individuals who worship God because we choose to do so (notice the implicit questioning of God's Lordship/authority in such a notion) stems precisely from the fact that we have been taught to be self-determined. Enlightenment autonomy has taught us we have the same kind of freedom as God Himself. Thus, we live in a world of "choices." Indeed, the focus on choice in contemporary ethics is largely due to our commitment to autonomy. Character development through patterning and formation (i.e., discipleship) is too dependent on others for our Enlightenment sensibilities. Likewise, anything external to our own rationality, such as Biblical revelation, is anathema to the Enlightenment principles of religion. In other words, like the historical critics of generations past who questioned the validity of the Biblical text, making its authority suspect, evangelicals now undermine Biblical authority by appealing to our own autonomous reason. We somehow feel we have the right to make choices, though we may not yet have the training to be capable of such choices. Certainly exceptions can be found to these tendencies. But the overall movement of the Enlightenment is directly opposed to anything like Biblical Christianity, that is, a formative community that functions as the church seems to have in the first century. To defend such Enlightenment notions seems perilous, at best, for a church that wishes to be faithful to its origins.
>
> As the modern church, we are hardly in any condition to contemplate what it means to be formed into the image of Christ. We have been taught that sanctification is a matter of being given enough information to afford us the opportunity to make good choices, the presumption being that we are innately good and will "naturally" choose the good if just left alone and given enough information, which is of course liberalism. "But we now have the Holy Spirit!!" some will object. My response is, "Yes we have the Holy Spirit, but He does not make us automatically competent." We still need to be taught how to pursue righteousness. It is not natural to our being to be holy people, even after the coming of

Domesticated Glory

It may sound outrageous to challenge the value of the common good. After all, isn't everyone supposed to be concerned about the welfare of his/her neighbor? While I certainly recognize the Christian duty to "love thy neighbor," I do not believe Jesus meant to elevate the welfare of society above His Kingdom message. In other words, pleas for Christians to direct their efforts toward support of the common good of all humanity assumes too much. The presumption underlying the common good is that all humanity shares a common destiny, perspective, and care for life in this world, i.e., liberalism. The Social Gospel made this presumption a commonplace belief amongst liberal churches, but it seems far removed from the Biblical intentions of loving neighbor. Certainly I am not opposed to showing concern and working for the benefit of our neighbors' well being. However, it seems that such has become the primary means for conveying Jesus's message of the Kingdom of God. We have centered the message of the Kingdom around what happens in this world—what happens in this life. The "good" that is common to all humanity is only a temporal good, in that it is limited to sustaining human existence prior to death. This is only a part of the Gospel message in Scripture, and a very limited part at that. Where is the promise of the coming Kingdom offered by Jesus throughout His ministry? Allow me to illustrate this point by addressing the place of Christians in government.

One might assume that I am opposed to any Christian involvement in government. On the contrary, I am very much in favor of it. However, I would ask that Christians act like Christians when working in positions of authority and representation. This means Christians speak the language of faith, seek conversion of those who do not yet recognize the Lordship

---

the Holy Spirit into our lives. Many evangelicals have adopted liberalism precisely by presuming that simply because we now have the Holy Spirit, we are able, without training, to naturally pursue the good. Such presumption lacks the insights of such secular thinkers as Aristotle and the words of the apostle Paul as he wrote to the Corinthians, "Be imitators of me, just as I also am of Christ" (1 Cor 11:1).

Of course the state realizes the power of training. In fact, the state is discipling our children every day on how to be good Americans. That is why the Pledge of Allegiance is so important in schools, even for the youngest of children. That is why the flag presides over even the most unlikely of events, like high school football games, etc. We are being trained by the state every day, only we fail to realize it. We have been blinded to the fact that in many subtle ways, the state has captivated our devotion. We hardly even question it when called on to die, or further, to kill other Christians, for the state. Politicians understand this. Patriotism is a rallying cry that can overcome even the deepest of divisions amongst factions in the government.

of Jesus over their lives, and act in a manner conducive to the character of Jesus. Obviously, this will be difficult in governmental positions, perhaps even impossible. It will certainly make it difficult to be elected. But I would not wish a position of compromise on any Christian, especially those in the public eye. Unfortunately, in much of Christian politics today, the culture war is about the culture, not the Gospel.

Lest anyone think that this study is meant to pillory certain people or groups for succumbing to the temptation toward kingdom building, I would like to point out that this temptation is not unique. One of the three temptations of Jesus in the wilderness centered on the establishment of an earthly kingdom in a manner distinct from God's will. Satan "took Him to a very high mountain, and showed Him all the kingdoms of the world, and their glory; and he said to Him, 'All these things I will give You, if You fall down and worship me.'" (Matt 4:8–9). Of course, we know Jesus's response. What is interesting about this temptation is that Jesus knew all the kingdoms of the world would one day be His, and their glory (cf. Isa 9:6–7; Rev 21:24, among others). The temptation for Him was to become their king through means quite the opposite of God's will. Satan is asking Jesus to bypass the rejection, humiliation, and shame of living as a servant, rather than a king, and finally dying as a criminal, crushed by His heavenly Father. The revealing prayers of Jesus in the garden demonstrate that He honestly desired His kingship to be revealed in a way other than by bearing the Father's wrath on the cross, but He desired the Father's plan above His own (Matt 26:36–46). The way of the world (i.e., the devil) may be rather enticing, and perhaps much easier, but it is never best.

Likewise, the disciples were allured by the coming of the kingdom in power and might (Mark 10:35–37; Luke 9:51–54). Even after Jesus had demonstrated that His way was going to be through a more humbling and non-revolutionary means, they still didn't grasp it. When faced by the resurrected Jesus, one of their questions that was recorded for us is "Lord, is it at this time You are restoring the kingdom to Israel?" (Acts 1:6). They still expected the kingdom to be immediate and physically present. They must have been dumbfounded when Jesus was lifted from their midst. Fortunately, they had the wherewithal to learn to live in the between times—without authority, without power, as "aliens" and "sojourners" (1 Pet 1:1; 2:11).

Likely, another strong temptation Jesus faced was similar to that presented by Satan, but from a different source. When Jesus was at the wedding at Cana, he was approached by His mother after the wine had run out. Many commentators understand her statement "They have no wine" (John 2:3) to be an indication that Jesus's and His disciples's presence at the wedding has caused an undue burden on the supply of wine. Therefore, she was requesting Him to use His supernatural powers to make more for the feast. This would have kept everyone happy and "saved face" for the host.[26]

There are two problems with this interpretation. First, the text gives no indication that the party is ending "early." It simply states that the wine has run out, which is likely how all wedding parties ended, whether short or long. The second problem is that this interpretation does injustice to Jesus's reply. When He says, "Woman, what do I have to do with you? My hour has not yet come" (2:4), this hardly seems a response to the question, "Could you make more wine?" It seems to be an even more incongruous interpretation given the fact that Jesus does make the wine. If Jesus is responding to the request to make more wine with a fairly emphatic "No!" then why does He turn right around and make the wine? This interpretation misses the point.

Instead, it seems best to understand Mary's request as a remembrance of the angels's and others's words at Jesus's birth and the inauguration of His ministry. A further affirmation likely would have been known by Mary and others through Jesus's baptismal event and perhaps His pronouncement of Himself as the Spirit-anointed one they were expecting (Luke 4:14–21). In other words, Mary knew who Jesus was and what He was meant to be—the Messiah of Israel. She knew that this man before her would be the One who would take the throne of David and rule over the land and its inhabitants. We should hardly blame her for expecting this wedding to be a good time for Jesus to reveal Himself as the Messiah. She knew well that Israel was still under the occupation of the Romans. In fact, only a few miles from Cana at the northern end of the sea of Galilee was a common site where Jews needed to pay a tax to pass

---

26. E.g., see Merrill C. Tenney, *John: The Gospel of Belief* (Grand Rapids: Eerdmans, 1976) 82–83; J. Ramsey Michaels, *John*, New International Biblical Commentary (Peabody, MA: Hendrickson, 1989) 46–47; Leon Morris, *The Gospel according to John*, New International Commentary on the New Testament, (Grand Rapids: Eerdmans, 1995) 156–60; George R. Beasley-Murray, *John*, Word Biblical Commentary (Waco: Word, 1987) 34–36. Beasley-Murray understands the reference to Jesus's "hour" as having eschatological significance, but does not incorporate it into his comments as well as he could have.

from one region into another. Many of the guests probably passed this site on their way to the wedding. The wine was running out at the wedding, meaning that the men were still, likely, rather boisterous and uninhibited. Undoubtedly, they were talking treasonously about their dislike of the Romans and ways to kick them out of Israel. Even if this was not the case, we can be sure many of the men from that region were about to leave the celebration. Remembering well that the One who was going to take Israel's throne was standing in their midst, Mary comes to Jesus and says to Him, "They have no wine." In other words, Mary seems to be saying, "The wedding is over and people are about to leave. This would be a good time for You to reveal who You are and begin to put into action Your plan for revolution." This would especially make sense directly following Jesus's baptism, since He now has been anointed by the Spirit to fulfill His role as Messiah (John 1:19-34). Such an interpretation makes Jesus's response intelligible, "Woman, what do I have to do with you? My hour has not yet come." Jesus is telling her that His rule is not to be revealed at this time, and His actions tell her that it is not going to be established by force.

Mary doesn't understand Jesus's words. She is still expecting the Messiah to come in the same manner all the other Jews were expecting. So, she turns to the servants to command them "Whatever He says to you, do it." (v. 5). She is commanding the servants to be at Jesus's beck and call. The question to ask is "What did she expect the servants to do?" In this more political interpretation I am giving, it would seem she expected the servants to be the ones who would gather the armaments for battle and who would run to other locations to alert people sympathetic with the revolution to gather themselves for war. The servants would be the ones who would naturally take on these duties, if for no other reason, because the men who would do the fighting were still somewhat incapacitated.

However, Jesus surprises her by extending the feast in a glorious way—with the best wine—rather than beginning a revolution by force. He demonstrates that His kingdom will come in an unexpected manner. He will come in glory to rule one day, but His kingdom is entering in a different way now. He does not accept the reins of earthly power from those who would prefer a king in the manner *they* wanted. Instead His rule, His peace, would be unlike anything they expected or could imagine. The lack of power in Jesus's kingdom at this first advent may be humiliating. His weakness may even be embarrassing. But then, His way is opposite the ways of the world (Mark 10:42–45). Truly, this is the Prince of Peace (Isa 9:6).

This may be an appropriate place to address the issue of pacifism, which will come up again in a later chapter. While it is true that Jesus's own approach in His first advent was rather pacifistic, or non-violent, such a construal of His message seems to miss the point. Certainly, He was advocating non-violence, but such non-violence is but an implication, or consequence, of His teaching; it is not the primary thrust of His teaching. Indeed, pacifism in itself is hardly virtuous. Instead, Jesus's primary message is peace: peace with God, and peace with one another. Only as we pursue peace with God and others can we truly *be* at peace and experience the right relationships God intended. Peace, especially peace with God, comes through the Gospel. Avoiding violence, or pursuing a non-violent stance toward others is but an implication of a Christian's primary devotion to peace. Pacifism is not an objective, per se. It is a consequence of our objective: pursuing peace. This is how Christians should be known, since God "gave us the ministry of reconciliation" (2 Cor 5:18).

CONCLUSION

Jesus Himself was constantly confronted with the option to rule now rather than later. His choice is a telling reminder to us that His Kingdom is "not of this world" (John 18:36). Though the church may anticipate the Kingdom in a very physical way, it is not the fulfillment of the Kingdom, since Christ is not physically present on His throne yet. This is not an escape from existence in the world; this is not "fundamentalist separationism"—quite the opposite. It is a call to an existence that reflects the power of witness, rather than the power of control. The Social Gospel movement's underlying flaw was its willingness to trade the power of the Gospel for moments of fleeting cultural optimism. Evangelicalism has become enchanted by similar liberal desires as it seeks safety and comfort in the life this world has to offer. This is a trade Jesus was consistently unwilling to make. We can accept no less from ourselves.

Liberalism is like a coin with two sides. On one side is the conclusion to leave antiquated approaches to Biblical doctrine behind; on the other side is the desire to emphasize specific doctrines that further an agenda adopted for reasons directed by the culture. Generally, in contrast to liberalism's dismissal of Scripture, evangelicals staunchly cleave to orthodox doctrines, according to our best understandings of what the doctrines are affirming. Unfortunately, the other side of the coin has become too enticing to resist. Some evangelicals have emphasized or revised doctrines to make them more compatible with political action and a cultural agenda. At the same time, while clinging tightly to fundamental doctrines like the deity of Christ and the inerrancy of Scripture, other "fringe" doctrines, like the church, have been left behind in favor of political action. Extra-biblical doctrines believed to be fundamental to our existence (e.g., Enlightenment notions of autonomy and freedom) have assumed a more primary role. This is true to such an extent that freedom, as it is defined in our post-Enlightenment context (i.e., the removal of all constraints), is deemed by many to be an ingredient of higher necessity for the existence of the church than are the internal workings of the church described in Scripture. In such a context, discipleship is reduced merely to teaching information.

Another illustration of our departure from orthodox belief pointed out in this chapter is the way in which orthodox doctrine is translated into "political-speak." The language of revelation that helps believers know what it means to live as God requires is easily being translated into (i.e., reduced to) the language of "traditional values" meant to effect moral change in the general populace. In other words, though couched in a commitment to orthodox doctrine, the goals of evangelical politics seem closely akin to a further implication of the Social Gospel. Evangelicals seem bent on making the world a safe place in which to be a Christian.

The problem in the church's relationship to the world and its government is finally not that the church is consciously choosing to follow after other gods. The problem is that the church no longer knows how to be the church, and thus feels compelled to look for other gods who carry more sway in the public square. The church is allowing the politics of America to take over its own claims on people's lives because the church has become meaningless as a body. It has become weak and is succumbing to the temptation to rule instead of follow, to reign instead of wait. The church no longer matters precisely because the church no longer exists as matter.

THREE

Faithful in Little . . . The Primacy of Person in Biblical Truth

IN OUR WESTERN WORLD, where truth is expected to be an objective statement or fact isolated from the bias of person and circumstance, Jesus's statement "I am the truth" leaves the contemporary (i.e., modern) reader perplexed. Typically, as moderns, we are drawn to reduce such a statement to the theological facts we believe are implied by it. In other words, we believe Jesus meant to say that His existence is representative of some overarching truth, making His incarnation a vehicle for some theological principle, whatever that principle might be. However, such a reduction misses the point and does serious damage to the context in which Jesus's words were meant to be understood. If Jesus is merely representative of some truth more absolute than He is, then His Lordship is compromised.

In the political struggle for attaining a defensible position for truth claims in the public square, many evangelicals have anchored themselves solidly to the clarity discovered in rationality.[1] They have championed the notion of objective truth that is verifiable and available to all rational creatures. In order to accomplish such objectivity, truth must be extracted from its context and laid bare to the bone of absolute, or universal, import. Only when factual statements or events have been freed from their circumstance and environment can they possibly qualify as a truthful representation of "how things really are." The material existence of life and

---

1. E.g., see J. P. Moreland's *Love Your God With All Your Mind* (Colorado Springs: NavPress, 1997). Though Moreland maintains a place for body and action, he develops the relationship between body and mind along the same lines as Descartes. The body is subjugated to the soul/mind in such a way that rationality is finally the superior (only?) way of knowing (65–73).

Faithful in Little ... The Primacy of Person

history are, consequently, seen as an encumbrance, or at best, as a mere medium for communicating some overarching or universal idea.

The reason for procuring agreement over what is true is discovered in the politics of power. Those who wish to prove absolute truth are certainly concerned with demonstrating truth for its own sake. However, this is not where it ends. Truth has political implications. If a universal truth can be discovered, then a consensus can be built. This consensus may amount to a moral code or an agreed upon standard of the relationships designed into government. On the other hand, it could be used to combat other factions vying for control over human history through the state. Whatever the case may be, we should not underestimate the political power of truth. It has power in both the private and public arena to such an extent that even God finally becomes subject to our notions of truth. Absolute truth is truth greater than any individual mind; instead, it is truth for *all* rational minds. It is finally one of a very few "ultimate" powers.

Note how truth in the scenarios described above is primarily information. Though the belief that information can convey or represent truth is not particularly new, Enlightenment thinkers so emphasized the notion that any other perspective of truth is now obscured. Two options remain for those who seek truth: objectivity or subjectivity. Those who believe in the literal revelation and interpretation of Scripture adamantly defend the objective nature of its truth claims. Those who wish to find value in their material existence emphasize how context influences the way statements and events are understood—subjectivity. The subjective truth seeker sees a plurality of understandings and meanings that leave the door open for interpretation, depending primarily on the circumstance of the interpreter. Here the individual's mind reigns supreme. What is true for me is not necessarily true for all, but I make it my truth by relativizing all other truth claims to my own. For objective renderings of truth to be discovered through the maze of historical circumstance, the seeker must carefully sort through the data for the single principle or statement representing the truth behind the circumstances. Subjective rendering allow historical circumstances a more formative role in determining truth for the individual. Neither pure objectivity nor pure subjectivity is an especially comfortable position for evangelicals. Though the champions of objectivity are often conservative and believe in a literal interpretation of Scripture, they find themselves in the unenviable position of defending Enlightenment rationalism and a model of moral training based primarily in information (i.e., Gnosticism).[2] Subjectivists, on the other hand, affirm a plurality of truth, leaving them with little claim to shared reality, nor do they find any meaning in the history of Jesus's life, death, and resurrection beyond what they invest in it. Of course, what both objectivists and subjectivists share is that they subject the supremacy of Jesus to human constructions. When human rationality reigns supreme, whether it be for all rational creatures (objectivity) or merely for my own individuated existence (subjectivity), Jesus is subsumed into a philosophical formulation of truth. This can be illustrated by observing that both ask the same question. Both want to know "What is the truth?" Though Scripture may presume an answer to this question, the Bible does not seem to dwell on the subject. Instead, Scripture focuses on something far more comprehensive and, at the same time, more penetrating. The more important biblical questions are: "Who is the truth?" and "What is faithful to the truth?"

ARE WE ASKING JESUS THE RIGHT QUESTIONS?

As the trial of Pilate's life was unfolding before him, he quizzed a rather silent Jesus. He could not have known the effects of his decision to crucify another "pretender" to the throne. The brief interaction he has with Jesus seems to be enough for him to decide Jesus's fate. His wish to please Jesus's critics must have made the decision to go against the evidence easier. Jesus was too much of a Messiah for Roman conscience, but not enough of one for Jewish ambitions. Thus, handing him over to be crucified satisfied all concerned.

In the course of Pilate's examination of Jesus, the conversation ends with a discussion of truth.

> Therefore Pilate entered again into the Praetorium, and summoned Jesus and said to Him, "Are You the King of the Jews?" Jesus answered, "Are you saying this on your own initiative, or did others tell you about Me?" Pilate answered, "I am not a Jew, am I? Your own nation and the chief priests delivered You to me; what have

---

2. I am here thinking specifically of Moreland's epistemological discussion of the soul and mind in his *Love Your God With All Your Mind*, 64–82. Though I have a healthy appreciation of mind and its place in epistemology, I fear Moreland's focus on mind as the primary, or even sole, avenue for gaining truth and knowledge leaves us in the problematic position of being *merely* thinking creatures. The parallel to Gnosticism is obvious. The minimization of body to a mere effect of the mind (69) leaves the reader wondering if bodies really are the simple machines Descartes envisioned all along. Certainly, this doesn't do justice to the holistic nature of a biblical anthropology.

You done?" Jesus answered, "My kingdom is not of this world. If My kingdom were of this world, then My servants would be fighting so that I would not be handed over to the Jews; but as it is, My kingdom is not of this realm." Therefore Pilate said to Him, "So You are a king?" Jesus answered, "You say correctly that I am a king. For this I have been born, and for this I have come into the world, to testify to the truth. Everyone who is *of the truth* hears My voice." Pilate said to Him, "What is Truth?" (John 18:33–38; emphasis mine)

On a textual level, it remains a question whether Pilate actually asked the question "What is truth?" It would seem more in character with his mocking tone and the moral climate of the day for Pilate to ask "Who is truth?" Jesus's use of the definite article in both of His references to the truth, and the absence of it in Pilate's question may indicate that Pilate is moving in such a direction, intending to generalize on the point already made by Jesus. The interrogative pronoun in Greek allows for many different renderings. Putting the question of "Who?" back to Jesus after He has just indicated His followers are "of the truth" (ultimately they are "of Him") seems the most appropriate response, if we believe Pilate was here trying to goad Jesus. Of course, the use of the neuter certainly makes "What" a plausible option. However, I have difficulty projecting a pluralistic question regarding the substance of truth back into the first century. "*What* is truth?" is a question for our century, not theirs.

Such musings about the translation do not solve the issue for us. Instead, they introduce questions that may point toward a paradigm shift in our understanding of the biblical perspective on truth. Such a paradigm shift is best introduced by asking a few questions of our history and the thought of Jesus's day: "Why is centering on the definition of truth interesting for the interpretation of this passage?" "What are some of the implications surrounding our interpretation?" "How was truth conceived in the first century and how might that conception differ from our own cultural understanding of truth?" Questions such as these open subjects deserving fuller treatment than is available here. Nevertheless, some discussion may allow us to begin mapping a strategy for answering these questions and more. Perhaps the best place to begin is with our own contemporary understanding of truth.

TRUTH IN RECENT HISTORY

The legal jargon and philosophical formulae of our age are meant to help clarify how the specifics of a historical circumstance are really representative of overarching ideas or principles. It is difficult for us to imagine a notion of truth other than what we find in statements and words, or numbers. In Aristotle's original formulation, truth is "to say of what is that it is, and of what is not that it is not."[3] While this statement seems simple, it conveys a fairly widely held conception of truth in antiquity as a direct relationship between language and nature. Language, and the subject's use of language, in this definition, is secondary to the nature of an object, such that truth is found in the accuracy of the language used to describe the object. The object remains primary in defining what may or may not be true regarding the same object. Such an understanding of truth changed drastically in the modern period as nature was slowly replaced by the reason of a subject, i.e., the rational mind. As Barry Allen summarizes,

> In modern philosophy, it is not nature or substance but the self-evident sameness of what is and what is affirmed when a subject is reflectively aware of itself as presently feeling, thinking, or apparently perceiving one thing and not another which demonstrates, against all skeptical doubt, the possibility in principle of a true-making sameness between thought and being. As Locke put it, "The Mind clearly and infallibly perceives each *Idea* to agree with itself, and to be what it is; and all distinct *Ideas* to disagree, i.e., the one not to be the other: And this it does without any pains, labour, or deduction; but at first view, by its natural power of Perception and Distinction." ... With this, the subject moves into the position formerly reserved for nature, and the way is open to Kant's thesis that nature is constituted by the spontaneous auto-affection of subjective reason.[4]

Thus, we have arrived at our current conception of truth in the modern world, where the subject (i.e., the individual's rational human mind) becomes the filter for truth. In recent decades, this conception has evolved into the postmodern pluralistic world, in which the subject becomes the

---

3. Aristotle, *Metaphysics*, in *The Basic Works of Aristotle*, edited by R. McKeon (New York: Random House, 1941) 1011b.

4. Barry Allen, *Truth in Philosophy* (Cambridge: Harvard University Press, 1993) 32. Allen is here quoting John Locke, *Essay Concerning Human Understanding*, edited by P. N. Nidditch (Oxford: Oxford University Press, 1975) IV.i.4.

determiner of truth. Modernism and postmodernism are not so distant when it comes to determining truth.

This albeit rather superficial historical review of truth is meant simply to lay a brief template for discussing truth as it may be discovered in the first-century historical work, the Bible. Specifically, we see that truth was previously associated with an external object, while now it is determined by the one who perceives the object. It would seem an easy question to answer, since the Bible is an ancient document. One would expect the Bible to offer truth as lying primarily, if not only, in an object or statements about an object. But the Bible does not seem to be so easily captured in a simple human construction. In the following paragraphs we will attempt to discover if the Bible conveys a monolithic presupposition of truth as correspondence between language and reality. Even further, could the subject possibly participate in truth without making truth relative to the subject? The discussion below means to demonstrate that defenders of truth as an abstract or absolute overarching principle may be, at best, missing some of the presuppositions regarding truth held by the authors of the original words of Scripture.

WHY HISTORY AND TRUTH DON'T FIT TOGETHER IN MODERNISM

Though much of this introduction has been couched in philosophical language, the argument is decidedly historical, in that what now passes for a defense of truth against postmodernism from a more theologically conservative viewpoint (i.e., objective absolutes) is, at times, bordering on a defense of modernism. As Doug Groothius has capably laid out for students of truth, objective truth is truth that may be regarded as untainted by human intervention or historical circumstance.[5] In other words, truth is discovered in claims that are overarching above any and all history; they are universal. Truth also may be regarded as "conformity to fact."[6] As J. P. Moreland and William Lane Craig point out,

> Two aspects of the Biblical conception of truth appear to be primary: faithfulness and conformity to fact. The latter appears to

---

5. Douglas Groothius, *Truth Decay: Defending Christianity Against the Challenges of Postmodernism* (Downers Grove, IL: InterVarsity, 2000) 60–82.

6. Ibid., 61, 62. Here Groothius defines the Biblical terminology for truth as primarily having to do with conformity to a fact(s) external to the person or circumstance.

involve a correspondence theory of truth. Arguably, the former may presuppose a correspondence theory. Thus faithfulness may be understood as a person's actions corresponding to the person's assertions or promises, and a similar point could be made about genuineness, moral rectitude and so forth.[7]

What such a notion of truth conveys is that truth, to be true, must be removed from any opportunity for history to invade or somehow shape the meaning conveyed regarding whether or not something is true. In other words, truth is not relative to any historical data or context. Biblical truth then is propositional, in the sense that the truth of revelation lies in the universal statements extracted from the story or descriptive narrative of Scripture.[8] At times, the proposition may be clear and easy, as in didactic literature. At other times it may be more obscure, as in parables or eschatological literature. However, what such an objective hermeneutic excludes, to its own detriment, is the emotive and formative power of the text itself. This is especially evident in ethics. The expectation is, of course, that propositional statements of principle or fact can easily be transformed into action through proper understanding and *subsequent* application. Unfortunately, this is precisely where the breakdown often exposes the flaws of relying on such a "trickle down" understanding of moral training. The linear nature of modern ethics—that right thinking *naturally* leads to right action—is now rightly seen as epistemologically and anthropologically suspect. In other words, to set this in the context of the history of philosophy, I would prefer to argue, along with Aristotle

---

7. J. P. Moreland and William Lane Craig, *Philosophical Foundations for a Christian Worldview* (Downers Grove, IL: InterVarsity, 2003) 131. I believe Moreland and Craig are exactly right to see truth according to two aspects. Unfortunately, they seem to miss the hierarchy that exists in the Biblical relationship of the two. Notice how they subsume faithfulness into correspondence such that it is dependent on a statement or promise, which may be isolated into a principle. Thus, faithfulness may be measured according to universals and is not left to any subjective interpretation. Accordingly, any claim to truth must be reducible to some proposition in order to be verifiable, or true. In contrast to this, Scripture seems to value the two aspects differently.

8. It is a worthwhile question to ask why the Scriptures were not given as a simple listing of propositions, if propositions carry truth more effectively or more precisely than narratives of historical circumstances and events. In regard to Jesus, it is further significant to note that we are given four different interpretive biographies in relation to His life. Perhaps this is more than simply the tradition of oral histories being transformed into written history. As will be discussed further below in regard to moral formation, perhaps God's revelation to His creatures was given in language that teaches in a way abstract principles cannot.

and the apostle Paul, that how we come to know holiness is more through imitation (i.e., discipleship) than it is through understanding first and *then* subsequently applying principles in action.⁹

In our modern scenario, where truth is primarily information, historical circumstance is to be suppressed or removed, as much as possible, in order to reveal the underlying principles, propositions or "facts." These facts may then be understood in a more general, or abstract, sense. Such a move is decidedly modern in theology as it supposes any religious truth must be removed from history in order to be truth. In philosopher Immanuel Kant's understanding with regard to religious language,

> [I]n the end religion will gradually be freed from all empirical determining grounds and from all statutes which rest on history and which through the agency of ecclesiastical faith provisionally unite men for the requirements of the good; and thus at last the pure religion of reason will rule over all, "so that God may be all in all."¹⁰

Though certainly most theologians would recognize the damage such a position does to the extremely historical nature of the Gospel, we nevertheless seem to subscribe to Kant's ideal for religious truth.¹¹ We look for the principles behind the text, or for the "point" the author of the text is trying to make. All the while, we believe the historical circumstance of the text is merely given for the sake of "couching" the abstract or universal truth underneath the circumstance. The logical end of such a strategy is finally to arrive at religious principles that bear no historical reference and contain only principles that could be deemed acceptable to any rational creature, i.e., liberalism.¹² It seems at times that evangelicals, in their drive

---

9. While Aristotle seems to argue that action is primary in ethics and Kant argues that thought takes priority over action, I wish to argue that the two, thought and action, are reciprocal in the development of moral character. In other words, they influence each other, rather than functioning in a linear fashion.

10. Kant, *Religion Within the Limits of Reason Alone*, trans. with an Introduction by Theodore M. Greene and Hoyt H. Hudson (New York: Harper, 1960) 112.

11. One need only look to our conception of the Gospel to see Kant's influence in action. We have transformed the Gospel into a body of information or knowledge, appealing primarily to reason as the locus of true belief. In many portrayals of the Gospel, belief in specific facts about the person and work of Jesus is what makes one a believer. In contrast, we must ask, "Was the biblical authors' definition of belief really so thin?"

12. Some may question whether such rationalism still exists amongst evangelicals. In other words, doesn't everyone now recognize the problematic nature of assuming a

to find the universal truth overarching the historical circumstance of Jesus's life are following a pattern of hermeneutics laid out a half-century ago by Rudolph Bultmann.

> [M]odern science does not believe that the course of nature can be interrupted or, so to speak, perforated, by the supernatural powers ... Modern men take it for granted that the course of history, like their own inner life and their practical life, is nowhere interrupted by the intervention of supernatural powers ... We must ask whether the eschatological preaching and the mythological sayings as a whole contain a still deeper meaning which is concealed under the cover of mythology. If that is so, let us abandon the mythological conceptions precisely because we want to retain their deeper meaning. This method of interpretation of the New Testament which tries to recover the deeper meaning behind the mythological conceptions I call *de-mythologizing*—an unsatisfactory word, to be sure. Its aim is not to eliminate the mythological statements but to interpret them. It is a method of hermeneutics.[13]

Evangelicals have rightly taken issue with Bultmann's dismissal of the supernatural in favor of the meaning behind the "myth." However, the parallel that seems to remain is simply this: just as Bultmann wished to reduce the text to a few absolute principles that resided behind it, so too

---

general rationality exists amongst humans such that we can appeal to reason with a justified expectation that anyone will understand specific theological claims? The popularity of such works as C. S. Lewis's *Mere Christianity* (New York: Macmillan, 1952) and the continued proliferation of evidentialist works in apologetics (e.g., William Lane Craig's *Reasonable Faith: Christian Truth and Apologetics* [Wheaton, IL: Crossway, 1994]) should demonstrate that evangelicals, like much of the unbelieving populace, rely on the notion of a general rationality in humanity. One could even place the debate over natural theology and natural law ethics here as further examples of the reign of reason in evangelical doctrine and public theology. Though I would agree that all humans bear a capacity for reason and can even come to a sense of agreement over right and wrong, such an approach to theology and ethics is highly reductionistic in regard to Christianity. It is precisely such an emphasis on the "common ground" Christians and non-Christians share that leads some non-Christians to believe they are Christian when they are not. Further, it leads some Christians to believe evangelism is a process of translating Christianity into the moral or economic language and doctrine of the world, creating political alliances wherever possible with others who may be willing to grant some level of agreement. This is indeed a dangerous, and perhaps even fatal, project for Christians. It transforms Christianity into just another secular philosophy, albeit a benevolent one. The value of general revelation is only rightly discovered within the purview of special revelation.

13. Rudolf Bultmann, *Jesus Christ and Mythology* (New York: Scribner, 1958) 15, 16, 18.

evangelicals are comfortable removing the text from its historical context. Certainly, evangelicals attempt to interpret the Scripture in light of the historical context, but in so far as we continue to look for some absolute, or overarching, teaching that summarizes the "point" of specific passages, we are not that different from Bultmann.

In the politics of truth, both evangelicals and liberals (Bultmann's denial of the supernatural is a vestige of his liberal commitments) seem committed to the notion that truth must be egalitarian to be true. In other words, anyone who is willing to simply look at the facts will be able to recognize the veracity of a rational statement or claim based on the facts in evidence. For truth to be universal, it must be *recognizably* true for all rational creatures. Of course, God's revelation becomes rather suspect at this point, since the apostle Paul indicates that some truths are "spiritually appraised" and are not available to the natural, or "unregenerate," person (1 Cor 2:14). Evangelicals seem loath to admit they hold to truths that are unavailable to all, since such an admission would place Christians on distinct grounding from unbelievers, perhaps even subjecting Christianity to minority status. In plain language, evangelicals are afraid of being labeled irrational, and they seek to establish their power in consensus. But have we compromised too much?

Paul seemed to have words of encouragement for this situation,

> [B]ut God has chosen the foolish things of the world to shame the wise, and God has chosen the weak things of the world to shame the things that are strong, and the base things of the world and the despised, God has chosen, the things that are not, that He might nullify the things that are, that no man should boast before God. (1 Cor 1:27–29)

No room exists for us to make claims of understanding beyond what God has revealed to humanity. Certainly, rationality can be a wonderful tool for understanding revelation, but even in our understanding, we have no room to boast. Our greatest achievement with regard to truth is not to conceive it in such a way as to make it available to anyone, believer and unbeliever alike. Instead, our greatest achievement is to worship in light of the world of revelation as God has portrayed it. Such "knowing" is far more than mere human rationality can grasp. It is "spiritually appraised" and is only available to those pursuing the character of holiness by imitating the life of Jesus described in Scripture and enfleshed in His followers; it is only available to those who wish to live the Gospel.

I am here leaving aside the problematic confidence modernists and evangelicals sometimes place in reason. One could easily develop a case for distrusting reason due to the fact it is always subject to the taint of sin, even in a regenerate person. Instead of pursuing this criticism of confidence in reason, I simply wish to point out that by making truth ahistorical, we are *a priori* deciding the history of Jesus is unimportant, even meaningless; it is merely a vehicle for the larger truth He represented. On this point, we should be mindful of the response mentioned previously by much of the liberal church at large in Nazi Germany. They were quite content with a *history-less* Jesus, instead transforming Him into a set of universal principles. Though no Evangelical can possibly go to this extreme, even though we may use the same method, we nonetheless do damage to the doctrine of the Incarnation as we understand the person of Jesus as *merely* representative of something greater than Himself. More specifically, Jesus's statement "I am the way, the truth, and the life" is deemed representative of the larger theological truth that it is only in Jesus we can be saved, which appears, at best, short-sighted.[14] Since Jesus spoke these words while subject to the material existence of the Incarnation, perhaps they deserve to be interpreted with His human existence as, at least, a part of the backdrop. While I wholeheartedly agree with the absolute nature of Jesus's statement (in other words, I fully affirm it is only through Him that anyone is able to come to the Father), I'm not convinced such an overarching principle is the only thing to which Jesus is referring here. I fear in the attempt to discover the overarching principle in Jesus's statement, we have lost an understanding of truth discovered in the culture of the first century and in Scripture itself.

Though it is, I believe, patently true that statements in Scripture are meant to be representative, that is, I believe they mean to communicate something about history, people, and God, I do not believe language should be limited to simple information. In other words, though I believe words convey particulars of circumstance well, we must be careful not to limit them merely to their relationship to reality. Words have more potency than simple representation. Likewise, they are more than just a contextualized narrative, or "game" to use Ludwig Wittgenstein's term.

---

14. Groothius, *Truth Decay*, 69.

Of course, the statements in Scripture are not necessarily always well understood. Metaphors and figures of speech are one thing, but misunderstanding or dismissing historical context can be quite another. By making truth the political battleground for validating the reality of Christian claims, we have translated truth in Scripture into mere information. In other words, I fear that as evangelicals have contended for a truth that may be found in the facts of nature, or in the abstract logic of objective reason, we have limited the description of language and truth in a way that does theological damage to the human aspects of Christology. Jesus did not say "I will show you the truth," or "I am representative of the truth." He said "I *am* the truth." What's more, the notion that truth is facts or statements does fundamental damage to biblical anthropology. A grand illustration of this can be seen in the way some Scriptural translations reduce the Hebrew term *labab* ("heart") in the Old Testament to "mind" in their rendering of certain passages, as though mind somehow represents human ontology in total.[15] Such a move ignores Jesus's comprehensive anthropology when he quotes the greatest command (Luke 10:27), Himself maintaining a distinction between heart and mind. Certainly the term may at times include and even emphasize the powers of reasoning; our problem is that we have limited reasoning exclusively to rationality. Our own Gnosticism is displayed in the way we limit truth to a specific genus of knowledge or understanding. Even further, it is displayed in the way we limit the significance of Jesus's human existence to the "representation" of theological ideas. To comprehend how we might overcome such a shift in our notion of truth limited to information, we must do a bit of "digging" into the cultural context surrounding Jesus's statement "I am the Truth." How would His audience have understood such a statement? How can we possibly understand Jesus's very being as truth, particularly as He existed as a human, rather than seeing His life as merely representative of the truth?

---

15. Though places certainly may arise where "mind" seems to capture the best rendering of "heart," I fear that translations too often reflect the cultural preference for such an Enlightenment influenced epistemology/ontology. E.g., see the New International Version's rendering of Ecclesiastes 7:25 and 8:9. Also, note how the word "spirit" in Isaiah 40:13 is rendered "mind." These may seem like merely issues of semantics. However, I prefer to discover, as closely as possible, the ancient epistemology/ontology, rather than project a modern epistemology onto Scripture.

JESUS AS THE TRUTH *OF* HUMANITY

In discussions of the biblical "definition" of truth, some have posited that the Scriptures do not give us a concise philosophical definition.[16] As a consequence, any definition we might think we have has been teased from the presuppositions of the texts in which truth is discussed or statements of fact are given. However, it seems the reason we find no definition of truth in Scripture may be because we are asking for the wrong type of definition. We are anachronistically asking the Scriptures to give us a definition that fits the modern rigors of philosophy and are ignoring or dismissing, or perhaps simply misunderstanding, the definition given us in plain language. When we anticipate a definition given in abstract or objective, rather than descriptive (i.e., historical), terms, our modern presuppositions betray us. Jesus said "I am the Truth!" Little attention has been given to how the culture of the first century would have understood such a statement about truth. Certainly, many histories of philosophy have been written with commentary on the understanding of truth that would have been held in various cultures during the first century. However, little discussion in the theological "truth war" of recent days has focused on the historical context of the Scriptures. When Jesus discussed truth, was He relying on the cultural understanding of truth at the time, or was He inventing something new?

Perhaps the best place to begin is with a few representative statements found in the New Testament where truth is specifically mentioned. The apostle John especially seems to enjoy the subject of truth. For the sake of space, references will be limited here to selections from his Gospel. Some of his references to truth include:

John 1:14: "And the Word became flesh and dwelt among us, and we beheld His glory, glory as of the only begotten from the Father, full of grace and truth."

John 1:17: "For the Law was given through Moses; grace and truth were realized (εγενετο) through Jesus Christ."

John 8:31–32: "Jesus therefore was saying to those Jews who had believed in Him, 'If you abide in My word, then you are truly disciples of mine; and

---

16. Groothius, *Truth Decay*, 60.

you shall know the truth (Truth?), and the truth (Truth?) shall make you free."

John 8:40, 44–45: "But as it is, you are seeking to kill Me, a man who has told (λελάληκα) you the truth, which I heard from God... You are of your father the devil, and you want to do the desires of your father. He was a murderer from the beginning, and does not stand in the truth, because there is no truth in him. Whenever he speaks a lie, he speaks from his own nature; for he is a liar and the father of lies. But because I speak the truth, you do not believe me."

John 14:6 (already mentioned): "I am the way, and the truth, and the life; no one comes to the Father but through Me."

John 16:13–14: "But when He, the Spirit of truth (genitive of apposition—'when He, the Spirit Who is the truth,'??), comes, He will guide you into all the truth; for He will not speak on His own initiative, but whatever He hears, He will speak; and He will disclose to you what is to come. He shall glorify Me; for He shall take of mine, and shall disclose it to you."

John 17:17: "Sanctify them in the truth; Thy word (Word?) is truth."

John 18:37b–38: "'You say correctly that I am a king. For this I have been born, and for this I have come into the world, to bear witness to the truth. Everyone who is of the truth hears my voice.' Pilate said to Him, 'What (Who?) is truth?'"

A simple listing of these verses is of little value; however, as one peruses the use of the word "truth" in each context, at least two distinct usages emerge. The first is the more modern understanding of truth as it is associated with universal reality. This usage has been mentioned earlier as "conformity to fact" or statements about external reality[17] Especially in John 8:40, truth is associated with language and statements that may be measured as to their conformity with other statements, words, objects, or events. This does not dissociate truth from its pragmatic display in the life of Jesus's audience, but it does seem as though He is pointing specifically to words and statements, which can be measured as more or less true. This is one of the usages of the word "truth" with which we are already

---

17. Ibid., 61, 62.

familiar, since this is the one typically touted as *the* definition of truth. As Groothius summarizes,

> [We have] sketched out the Biblical view of truth. At its heart is the claim that truth is what represents or corresponds to reality. Put differently, a true statement connects with the reality or facts it describes. Or so the Bible teaches.[18]

Interestingly, Jesus seems to imply in John 8:44–45 that the truthfulness of His statements should be measured by His own relationship to the Father. To make clearer what He is saying, by way of contrast, He explains that the falsehood of the devil's statements is determined according to his character, rather than the content of his specific statements. The apostle John makes this association of truth to character again in his first epistle when he exhorts his readers, "Little children, let us not love with word or with tongue, but in deed and truth. We shall know by this that we are *of the truth* (Truth?), and shall assure our heart before Him." (1 John 3:18–19; emphasis mine). A constant theme throughout this epistle by John is the assurance of true belief secured by being correctly aligned with the commandments of Christ—"abiding" in Christ. Such "abiding" seems to be a synonym for being "of the truth." In other words, truth appears to be enacted as much as, or more than, it is comprehended. John confirms such a notion in his first epistle where he teaches that those who lie do not have the truth *in* them (1 John 1:8, 10; 2:4; emphasis mine). One might think this to be a reference to a prior understanding of truth subsequently applied in action. However, it may be just as plausible, and perhaps more plausible, to understand John to be making a reference to character as it is reflected in ongoing action. In such an understanding, John would then consider truth to be a mark of the human character, rather than a statement of fact or principle. John is inclined to think of truth as something to be practiced, perhaps even limiting his primary reference to truth as what may be seen in action, rather than simply what someone says. "If we say that we have fellowship with Him and yet walk in the darkness, we lie and do not practice the truth; but if we walk in the light as He Himself is in the light, we have fellowship with one another, and the blood of Jesus His Son cleanses us from all sin" (1 John 1:6–7). Even the statement of fact or principle here seems to be subjected to an action of "practicing" or "doing" the truth. John maintains a very dynamic

18. Ibid., 83.

Faithful in Little ... The Primacy of Person

understanding of truth, even when it is associated with statements of fact or language. Biblical truth is more than facts or ideas, though such are certainly included. Instead, truth in Scripture often is associated primarily with the character of the person speaking.

With such an understanding of truth so prominent in John's writings, it appears as though perhaps a second distinct, though not unrelated, description of truth is being presented in the words and statements used by Jesus and others in Scripture. Further, Enlightenment distractions may have caused modern scholars to over-emphasize what first-century biblical authors may have considered a secondary aspect of truth. In other words, we may, today, have it backwards in that we emphasize abstract notions of truth over truth associated with action and character. Such an understanding of truth is made more explicit in statements such as John 1:17, where truth is said to have been εγενετο—"realized" or perhaps better, "came into being" in Jesus Christ. Such an association of truth with a person may seem confusing, but would help explain more fully statements about Jesus being "full of grace and truth," and His own claim to *be* the truth. Understanding truth as associated primarily with a person may also give us insight into John 4:23–24. When Jesus says that God is seeking worshipers who "worship in spirit and in truth," this may be a reference to character rather than to knowledge. Perhaps Ludwig Wittgenstein was not so original when he said

> No one can speak the truth; if he has still not mastered himself. He cannot speak it;—but not because he is not clever enough yet.
>
> The truth can be spoken only by someone who is already at home in it; not by someone who still lives in falsehood and reaches out from falsehood towards truth on just one occasion.[19]

As a point of fact, a stronger case for the relationship of truth to character could likely be made from Old Testament theology and its influence over the biblical authors. Though we would need to substantiate our observation from actual uses of the word in the OT text, it is interesting to note that the very word for truth in the OT, *'emet*, can also be translated as "faithfulness," implying truth may be seen in the light of the person making the statement as much as in the statement itself. In other words, the boundaries between the statement made by a person in the OT

---

19. Ludwig Wittgenstein, *Culture and Value*, trans. by Peter Winch (Chicago: University of Chicago Press, 1984) 35e.

and the person's character or reputation seem rather blurred. Perhaps this explains why God chooses to judge actions rather than knowledge.

JESUS AS TRUTH *FOR* HUMANITY

Imitation of God in the first century before Jesus may seem like something more remote, given the Jews's concern for protecting God's character. When Jesus made claims of being like His Father, the Jews constantly picked up stones to stone Him. However, Jesus was obviously not outside Scriptural boundaries. Indeed, Jesus makes claim that we should become like God when, in the Sermon on the Mount, He proclaims we "are to be perfect, as [our] heavenly Father is perfect" (Matt 5:48). Such a notion from Old Testament theology is also not lost on Peter, who recalls the command of Leviticus to "Be holy, for I am holy" (1 Pet 2:16). The purchase of noting this notion of imitating God in the Old Testament and in Jesus's teaching is simply to demonstrate that Jesus's expectation His disciples would follow, or imitate, Him is consistent with the notion that they would, in turn, become imitators of, or even become like, God the Father as well. Jesus's own life may, in this sense, be considered an enactment of the character of the Father in the only realm in which human knowledge is found: the material realm. Therefore, when Jesus states that He *is* the truth, He is saying that He is the embodiment, the imitation, the perfect representation of the Father (cf. John 1:18; Heb 1:1–3). "Bearing witness to the Truth" (cf. John 5:31ff.) must mean more than simply "talking about" the truth! This is His clear response to Philip only moments after saying He *is* the Truth, "He who has seen Me has seen the Father" (John 14:9). By no means does such a notion do damage to the deity of Christ, since it is easily complementary with Jesus's own self-abasement (*kenosis*—Phil 2:5–11) for the sake of the Father's glory. Jesus embodies all the supreme characteristics of God the Father, yet He does so in His material existence as a human.

Of course, the wonderful thing about claiming that truth is discovered in the person of Jesus is that such a theological move answers the question of subjectivity. If I were to say that truth is discovered in any person, then truth becomes relative to the human qua human. Thus, truth is totally subjective. This is what many evangelicals are, rightly, fighting against. However, to say that truth is discovered in the person of Jesus allows us still to find a material definition (i.e., description) of truth that can be perceived on a sensory level (i.e., material, historical). Yet at the same time, this is no ordinary person. The person of Jesus, as the perfect God-man, becomes the archetype for all humanity, and for all truth. Truth then is relative to the human qua Jesus, who is universal truth Himself. Universal truth is maintained, only its locus is found primarily, if not only, in the person of Jesus. Jesus is absolute truth and is not relative to theoretical constructions or conceptions of truth that transcend Him. He is the universal and absolute revelation of God. In other words, no theory of truth is absolute, in principle, over Jesus. Jesus, Himself, is *the* definition of truth, making Him a larger category than philosophical notions of truth. No abstract notion of truth resides above Him or prior to Him, to which He can only point as He attempts to represent it. Instead, He is the measure of truth. Unfortunately, our modern philosophical defense of truth as overarching all history and subjectivity has placed truth in a position above Him, such that we simply use Jesus to confirm an *a priori* notion of truth found in objective reason. To place Jesus in subjection to a theory of truth, though He certainly made use of such theories, is to create a context in which Jesus becomes relative to human rationality, even relative to the finite human creation of a definition of truth (i.e., idolatry). But Jesus is the most absolute and universal definition of truth we can have!! Allow me to demonstrate further how Jesus has supremacy over all theories and human constructions.

Four hundred years ago, René Descartes said, "I have always thought that two issues—namely God and the soul—are chief among those that ought to be demonstrated with the aid of philosophy, rather than theology."[20] Following in line with Descartes' method of reducing knowledge to only the thinking subject, we have since added to the list. We now seem to believe epistemology, ontology, and all foundations for knowledge, amongst other things not addressed directly in Scripture, belong primarily to philosophy. This can be seen especially in the debate between foundationalists and non-foundationalists. The foundationalist, especially, sees foundations as secure only if they can be grounded in a rational scenario. Such is our dissatisfaction with the language of Scripture. Such is our discontent with the Incarnation. The foundationalist believes we can, and should, achieve something called "objective truth" *so that*

20. René Descartes, "Meditations on First Philosophy," in *Discourse on Method and Meditations on First Philosophy*, 3rd ed., trans. Donald A. Cress (Indianapolis: Hackett, 1993) 47.

we might establish the veracity of Jesus (or any other theological truth claim) on the basis of the evidence.[21] The problem with such a move is obvious. Theological truth, including Jesus, becomes *relative to* the "facts" overarching history. Subjecting revelation to the merely rational has been the methodology of liberalism for generations now, as they understood Scripture in light of the laws of nature. Defenders of the Enlightenment have simply adopted the same method with a more conservative tone. What is most interesting about this shift is the parameters for establishing truth are not revelational; they are now the philosophical presuppositions supposedly grounding revelation. Revelation is being domesticated by the very foundations meant to prop it up. This is obviously no longer just a philosophical issue; it is clearly a critical theological issue. I have a feeling the apostle Paul would ask us the question of 1 Corinthians 1, "Where are those who are willing to be called foolish, even look foolish, for the sake of our Lord and His Gospel?"

Another way of putting the matter may be to ask, "Who gets the glory?" It seems clear from Scripture that all things, including creation and history, are meant to reflect the glory of God back onto His reputation. He enacts the activities of life in the historical context of the world around us so that His honor might be magnified. The problem with "universal" or absolute truth constructed on a rational foundation is precisely that it is contextless. Its strength is also its downfall. In other words, truth is true without reference to anything else, including God's revelation of Himself in word and person. This is theologically problematic, because consequently, universal truth *is* its own glory. It has reference to nothing and no one else.[22] Therefore, even God Himself stands outside of truth's claims to honor. Certainly someone may wish to claim that universal truth can honor God by finally being shown to be a product of His making: "All truth is God's truth." However, this does not answer the problem of whether truth has glory independent of God's revelation. Truth that is abstractly universal, that is, truth that exists regardless of the subjectivity of God's creation and eventual Incarnation, is finally still outside of God's

---

21. R. Scott Smith, "Post-Conservatives, Foundationalism, and Theological Truth: A Critical Evaluation," *Journal of the Evangelical Theological Society* 48 (2005) 362.

22. Of course, the irony of absolute truth is seen in the way it remains relative to human reason or logic. Human reason is still a historically contextualized reality. Thus, such universal statements require constant restatement or revision, even if only due to the evolution of language.

Faithful in Little ... The Primacy of Person

domain. Any glory it may attribute to God is limited to the interpreter, or the one who says that such truth is honoring to God. However, one might just as easily say universal truth owes its glory to another, e.g., the one who discovered it. In such a context, God's glory itself is finally subjective. The allure of philosophical knowledge has distracted us from the only locus of truth that is wrapped in the honor rightly due the Lord of truth. Ultimately, He is the truth and to separate some notion of truth from His revelation of Himself is to create a god of His affects, which is idolatry.

Bringing the conversation back to the level of Jesus as truth *for* humanity, to say that I have truth within me is simply another way of saying my life is parallel to, or an imitation of, Jesus. The question, then, becomes a question of faithfulness, rather than an abstract question of correspondence. Truth is not subjective, since one can be more or less faithful in his/her imitation of Jesus. In other words, one can be more or less true. Truth is by no means arbitrary, since it depends on the life of Jesus. So then, Pilate's question, "What is truth?" is a rather meaningless question for believers. Our concern is not about some abstract notion. On the contrary, our concern is "Who is the truth?" Further, as we aim to become truth ourselves, we are not arbiters of what is true or false (we are not pluralists). We are called instead to answer the question "Are our lives faithful to His?" In other words, "Are our lives true?" To use Jesus's words, "Are we 'of the Truth'?" (John 18:38).

We have been convinced that abstract notions of truth are prior to the enactment of truth. In such a scenario, we come to know truth first by understanding statements, then we enact those statements in subsequent actions. In such a "trickle down" notion of epistemology, principles and statements of truth are like wooden limbs we carve into arms and legs. Like Geppetto with his little wooden puppet Pinocchio, we pray these statements of truth will somehow come to life, if only we play with them long enough, or imagine them to be real. But our creations are never more than wood and strings. They merely imitate flesh and blood. By abstracting ourselves from the messiness of history, we find ourselves, finally, with little more than information. Oh certainly, we need limbs that move and joints that are flexible, like those of the wooden puppet—information is still necessary. But we need limbs that are alive, not ones that merely imitate life. We expect information to constitute knowledge and change lives, when in fact it takes another life to change a life. Jesus chose His disciples first and foremost "so that they might be with Him" (Mark 3:14). We need leaders in our churches who embody the life of Jesus, so that we may see His life in living flesh and follow (1 Cor 11:1). We are expecting the principles to do the job of the human. When we expect information to effect moral change through mere understanding, the incarnation becomes nothing more than a nice idea in theological dress.[23] Jesus's enfleshment doesn't really matter in this scenario. It's only the information or knowledge that's behind the incarnation that matters.

CAN TRUTH STILL BE TRUE?

Of course, such a theological scenario as outlined above probably raises more questions than it answers. For the sake of clarification, it may be good to illustrate how one might answer a very pointed question about the relationship of truth, language and character. Hopefully such illustrations can allow us to bring the discussion full circle. So what about the question: "Isn't a claim still true if someone is unfaithful, yet makes a true statement such as 'God is good'?"

What should be obvious to us here is that the presumption behind the question is as important as the question itself. This is actually not a question about veracity as much as it is a question about history. What is being asked is "Can we not separate the statement from the person making the statement and evaluate the statement on its own merits (i.e., objectively)?" The answer I would give is that we have done this for at least two hundred years, but this is not the way in which the NT deals with the question of truth. Truth is wrapped up in the interplay between action and thought in such a way that statements are not understandable apart from who makes them. Thus the NT focuses on the person as much as, or more than, the statement, making suspect any statement made by an untruthful person. Notice some of the statements in Scripture in which we find evaluation of character to be the mark of veracity:

Matthew 7:15–16: "Beware of the false prophets, who come to you in sheep's clothing, but inwardly are ravenous wolves. You will know them by their fruits. Grapes are not gathered from thorn bushes, nor figs from thistles, are they?"

---

23. I am intentionally using the language of Plato here (idea = form), since I believe modern Gnosticism is a parallel to the Gnosticism of the neo-Platonists of the early centuries of the church.

James 2:14: "What use is it, my brethren, if a man says he has faith, but he has no works? Can that faith save him?"

1 John 1:8: "If we say that we have no sin, we are deceiving ourselves and the truth (Truth?) is not in us."

To ask for the statement to stand on its own is to divorce theology from history, which is of course what liberalism has trained us to do. To remove a statement from its context (i.e., the speaker) is to assume that an external standard exists apart from the speaker by which we can measure the truthfulness of the statement. Certainly, Scripture exists as an external standard, but it doesn't stop there. We have also embraced reason as equally authoritative. The greater problem with such an approach arises when we attempt to do the same to Jesus. We would rather claim that Jesus really meant to say He "represented the truth," as though truth were somehow external to Himself as well. When we do this, we establish an objective authority external to Jesus by which His veracity is measured. The obvious question then is: "Which one is really God? Is it Jesus or the standard by which we measure Jesus?" Our external standards have become our idols, and we consistently subordinate God's supreme sovereignty under them.

CONCLUSION

When we ask "What is the truth?" and are given an answer that points us in the direction of Jesus rather than some abstract notion, we are dissatisfied because such an answer seems uncertain or arbitrary (i.e., relative). On the contrary, such an answer is as solid as we can get. Our dissatisfaction with the answer is a telling part of the problem. We have been convinced of what answer is acceptable and our criteria for truth have been formed by a culture that demands this answer be devoid of history or context (i.e., Kantianism). In other words, we have false expectations of what our knowledge should be. We, like Kant, have become convinced that Christian knowledge is knowledge for everyone, believer and nonbeliever alike, since "all truth is God's truth." Unfortunately, we are looking for truth outside the parameters established by revelation. We have come to believe that truth, to be true, must be obvious to any rational mind (who is the real pluralist here?). In the final analysis, "all truth *is* God's truth"; we have simply forgotten how to tell God's truth God's way.

In other words, we've been coerced into believing God's truth is better expressed in the terms of rationalism. This is not to say that God's truth is irrational, though it may be to the world (1 Cor 1:18–31). It is to say that its rationality is based in an uncompromising language of belief. Jesus is the true rationality; we should not wish to reduce Him to language acceptable to all. I say "reduce" here intentionally, for what we are doing is transforming special revelation into general revelation. We have come to believe we must translate the language of God into the language of man so anyone can grasp it. Unfortunately, such a Christian theology has become but another form of humanism, albeit a benevolent one. But the climax of special revelation, indeed the climax of all revelation is found in the person of Jesus, not in what He represented or symbolized. He, Himself, is the supreme Truth for mankind. Oh, that we would have the lives to be able to understand such truth, and the character to be truth and speak truth to one another.

I would like to close our discussion of truth by quoting a church father whose words seem written only decades ago. If we didn't know that he wrote only a few centuries after Jesus's resurrection, I fear we would all too easily dismiss him today as just another postmodern voice. However, his pre-modern sentiments attest to precisely what is lacking in the church today. Almost two millennia ago, Athanasius warned his readers:

> But for the searching and right understanding of the Scriptures there is need of a good life and a pure soul, and for Christian virtue to guide the mind to grasp, so far as human nature can, the truth concerning God the Word. One cannot possibly understand the teaching of the saints unless one has a pure mind and is trying to imitate their life. Anyone who wants to look at sunlight naturally wipes his eye clear first, in order to make, at any rate, some approximation to the purity of that on which he looks; and a person wishing to see a city or country goes to the place in order to do so. Similarly, anyone who wishes to understand the mind of the sacred writers must first cleanse his own life, and approach the saints by copying their deeds. Thus united to them in the fellowship of life, he will both understand the things revealed to them by God and, thenceforth escaping the peril that threatens sinners in the judgment, will receive that which is laid up for the saints in the kingdom of heaven.[24]

---

24. Athanasius, *The Incarnation of the Word of God*, trans. by A Religious of C.S.M.V. S.Th. (New York: MacMillan, 1947) ¶57.

FOUR

If these Become Silent, the Rocks Will Cry Out

The Public Nature of God's Glory

WE LIVE IN AN era of great freedoms: freedom of religion, freedom of speech, freedom of the press, a free conscience. Such freedoms are laudable in their intentions and, in many cases, their application. However, as the well-worn military cliché makes clear, freedom is never free. Such a sentiment points to the simple fact that freedom bears a price. That price is often measured in body bags and national debt. Precious lives of family members are the price paid for the rights Americans hold dear. But this is not the only price paid for the individual's right to believe whatever he/she wants. Along another vein, let us take a moment to ponder the theological price paid for religious freedom by those whom it affects. The theological price is not a reference to those who are persecuted for their faith or the freedom of their conscience; this would still be a physical price. Instead, in order to maintain a consistent freedom of religion, American Christians must live with the reality of pluralism in the west and the compulsion for Christians to support a pluralistic stance in the name of the freedom of belief. This type of freedom costs us something. Freedom of religion relies upon various coercive influences in order for freedom to remain. In other words, tolerance is the price all Americans pay for the sake of maintaining religious freedom. Though pluralism seems, on most occasions, a peaceful means to keep prevailing influences at bay, pluralistic powers could, in any era or political administration, attempt to enforce what may now only appear as a "strong bias" against the exclusive claims of Scripture. Pluralism itself could attempt to assert itself as the primary religious virtue. Perhaps, such enforcement of bias may even occur *in the name of* religious freedom. What exactly would it look like for a political entity to enforce freedom of religion?

This chapter will not address the political value of maintaining an ecumenical ambiguity amongst views vying for epistemological high ground—i.e., we will not attempt to assess the value of tolerance. Nor will we attempt to tease out the varied voices intent on taming Christian claims to exclusivity. Instead, we will examine briefly why religion in the West depends on the notion of privacy, which is inherently pluralistic, and how contrary such privacy is to the Biblical understanding of glory. God's glory is public and is meant to be proclaimed in every corner of the world. For Christians to acquiesce toward privacy or pluralism is tantamount to a defamation of God's reputation. Christians must deny the temptations to be silent or to translate their language of praise into a more palatable secular language of "rights" or "values," or worse, mere suggestions of value, for the sake of public participation. If we are to be scorned and hated for beliefs that run counter to Western privacy and pluralism, at least let us be scorned and hated for the right things.

KEEP YOUR OPINIONS TO YOURSELF!

The right to privacy dominates much of our public conversation about religion and morality. It's unclear whether people demand this right due to a fear of looking foolish if proved wrong about their beliefs, or perhaps it is due to embarrassment about what they believe deep down or their "sexual preferences." People seem to become uneasy when reminded that there is no place we can hide from God, not even our thoughts (Psalm 139:2–4). It is certain that people would wish to hide from God, if that were at all possible. Sin has always accompanied a craving for the camouflage of darkness. On the other hand, perhaps privacy is due to the need to prepare our thoughts before displaying them for public scrutiny. Along these lines, we believe it best to hold our tongue until we can say something useful and defensible. In other words, we simply appreciate the opportunity to maintain a bit of silence until we are prepared to say something we believe is meaningful to the conversation. Whatever the cause, many reasons likely exist for the vehement defense of personal privacy. We feel compelled by some emotion or bolstered by some personal reason to maintain the privacy of our thoughts. Privacy of this sort is a kind of personal ownership over our thoughts and words. This personal ownership rests on the deeper foundation of a political right inherent to being a participant in the public nature of democracy. I am distinguishing

If These Become Silent, the Rocks Will Cry Out

here between a personal sense of privacy and the political right to privacy, though the two are obviously connected. The compulsion for privacy and the political necessity for privacy in the West seem to be due to two different influences. As mentioned, the desire for privacy may be due to personal fear, embarrassment, or public preparedness. On the other hand, the necessity for privacy politically is due to fears of coercion and the public necessity of freedom from all constraints. Though both forms of privacy are equally powerful and authoritative, it is the latter that deserves attention in light of the political publicity God wishes for Himself.

When the American founders began considering how best to govern people without usurping the values of personal freedom, they turned within to justify the means of control. The human conscience must reign supreme, if people are to be given the right to believe freely and without pressure from king or church. The First Amendment's history was a decisive effort to frame the language of law in such a way as to protect individual liberties and the right to choose without fear of repercussions.

James Madison and Thomas Jefferson drew specific attention to the necessity for religion to be subject only to "the dictates of conscience."[1] As Jefferson once commented, "No man can form his faith to the dictates of another. The essence of religion consists in the internal persuasion of the mind."[2] Madison proposed language for the First Amendment outlining the belief that individual freedom and the right to choose religious belief were so intertwined that they must be held in union under the fledgling Constitution.

> The civil rights of none shall be abridged on account of religious belief or worship, nor shall any national religion be established, nor shall the full and equal rights of conscience be in any manner, or on any pretext, infringed ...
>
> No State shall violate the equal rights of conscience or the freedom of the press ...[3]

---

1. James Madison, *Memorial and Remonstrance Against Religious Assessments*, (1785), sections 1, 4, and 15, reprinted in Lenni Brenner, ed., *Jefferson & Madison on Separation of Church and State: Writings on Religion and Secularism* (Fort Lee, NJ: Barricade, 2004) 68–73.

2. Thomas Jefferson, "Notes on Religion," in *The Writings of Thomas Jefferson*, ed. by Paul Leicester Ford, 10 vols. (New York, 1892–1899) 2:101.

3. James Madison, *Proposed Amendments to the Constitution, House of Repre-sentatives* (June 8, 1789), as reprinted in Lenni Brenner, ed., *Jefferson & Madison on Separation of Church and State: Writings on Religion and Secularism* (Fort Lee, NJ: Barricade, 2004) 119.

Madison seems to be relying heavily here on John Locke's (1632–1704) formulation of the relationship of conscience to God first, and only subsequently to human laws. Cf. John Locke, *A Letter Concerning Toleration*, ed. by Patrick Romanell (New York: Liberal Arts, 1955) 48. For a more complete discussion of the ensuing debate and conclusions, see Martha C. Nussbaum, *Liberty of Conscience: In Defense of America's Tradition of Religious Equality* (New York: Basic, 2008) 72–114; and L. John Van Til, *Liberty of Conscience: The History of a Puritan Idea* (Phillipsburg, NJ: P. & R., 1972) 157–83.

Certainly Madison and Jefferson were not particularly original in their thoughts. Not only were both aware of Locke's thought, much of their thought regarding conscience and natural rights as coordinate with divine law had already been documented in Samuel Adam's *The Rights of the Colonists* (1772). Since the language used in founding documents is that of Madison and Jefferson, we will focus on their wording. However, historically speaking, they are conceptually indebted to several previous sources. In this sense, both may be better understood as summarizing the thoughts of colonial leadership, rather than originating the concepts finalized in America's founding documents.

It is pertinent to point out that in Adam's *Rights of the Colonists*, he seems to rely on Justice William Blackstone (1723–1780) for his conception of natural rights endemic to human nature, yet given by God. The question, of course, is "Who is the God who gives rights to humans?" It may seem obvious to answer that it is the God of the Bible. This may especially be the case for Blackstone, given the fact that the anthropology of natural rights for Blackstone is Lockean as it depicts man in his "state of nature," which Locke associated with original creation and a Biblical sense of egalitarianism. (Cf. Jeremy Waldron, *God, Locke, and Equality: Christian Foundations in Locke's Political Thought* [New York: Cambridge University Press, 2002].) However, two contrasting emphases seem to be at play in Locke's language and the American colonists's use of it. First, the giving of rights seems more associated with an Enlightenment conception of the way in which God created humanity, rather than any Biblical language regarding rights or the inherent capacities of humanity. Though Locke certainly has a point regarding equality associated with Adam and Eve, this by no means implies a Creator—creation relationship in which conscience is raised to a level of authority equal to that of divine revelation (such authority seems implied by Madison's conception of conscience and religious liberty). Madison and other founders seem to have accommodated theology to their culture on this point. Second, it is notable that the crafters of America's founding documents rejected the religious tests proposed by more conservative Christian voices of the time. For instance, William Williams proposed an alternative preamble to the Constitution, requiring a more resolute commitment to faith and the following of God. His wording fell short of a clear call to commitment to Christ, but was nonetheless overt in its call to faith in God. (See Frank Lambert, *The Founding Fathers and the Place of Religion in America* [Princeton: Princeton University Press, 2003] 236–37.) It was obviously not included in the final language of the Constitution. Indeed, it does seem somewhat odd that a Christian nation should avoid any specifically Christian language in its founding documents. The American documents had obviously moved far beyond Locke, even as limited as he was in his reference to Christianity, and any clear connection to Scripture. Perhaps the *Treaty of Peace and Friendship between the United States of America and the Bey and Subjects of Tripoli of Barbary* (1796) gave an accurate assessment in its claim that "the government of the United States is not in any sense founded on the Christian Religion."

If These Become Silent, the Rocks Will Cry Out

The final version of the Amendment was slightly different, but the point remained that religion was solely a matter of individual conscience.

This study is not meant to challenge the political necessity for religion to be individualized in the context of a democratic state. The value and appropriateness of such a necessity deserves Biblical scrutiny, but is outside the scope of our intentions here. Instead, our need is to focus on one of the implications of making religion a matter of individual conscience: all religious beliefs are thereby privatized to the level of personal opinion. Certainly the opportunity may still exist to share beliefs publicly and even to gather for the sake of celebrating beliefs held in common. However, in the end, all beliefs are left at the level of personal preference and individual choice. A plurality of beliefs, each held by individuals without fear of repercussion was the intentional design of the founders. The diversity of the settlers and the need to draw on differing sources demanded recognition of all participants. John Adams recounted the manifold makeup of the patriots who all believed they had a stake in securing freedom. Indeed, their own personal freedom of belief was at stake.

> There were among [those in the army], Roman Catholicks, English Episcopalians, Scotch and American Presbyterians, Methodists, Moravians, Anabaptists, German Lutherans, German Calvinists, Universalists, Arians, Priestleyans, Socinians, Independents, Congregationalists, Horse Protestants and House Protestants, Deists and Athiests; and Protestants que ne croyent rien [Protestants who believe nothing].[4]

Jefferson crafted the renowned Virginia Act for Establishing Religious Freedom in such a way as to open the door for complete freedom of religion. He went beyond John Locke's previous doctrine of toleration and opened the door for freedom of belief for all, including "the Jew, the Mohometan, and the Hindoo."[5]

---

4. Cited in *The Adams-Jefferson Letters: The Complete Correspondence between Thomas Jefferson and Abigail and John Adams*, ed. by Lester Cappon, 2 vols. (New York: Simon & Schuster, 1959) 2:339.

5. Thomas Jefferson, "Autobiography," *Writings of Thomas Jefferson*, Ford, 1:62. Locke argued that only religious groups who promoted public toleration of individual voices should be allowed any influence or place in society. This ruled out any group subject to specific authorities over the individual (e.g., Roman Catholics). Jefferson went further than Locke by putting all religious groups on equal footing, even those who promoted authoritative voices in their midst (Roman Catholics) and those who did not adhere to orthodox Christian doctrine (Jews and Quakers). Jefferson promoted equal place for all groups, so long as they remained individually voluntaristic.

Domesticated Glory

As an aside on this subject, it seems rather ironic than American evangelicals should be surprised by or incredulous about the attractiveness of pluralism today in our midst. Pluralism is blamed for the drift in America away from its Christian roots or foundations. However, pluralism was in the very fabric of American religious freedom from the start. In order for freedom to have its effect for the individual, a plurality of beliefs must be not merely tolerated, but promoted. Freedom in America has always been the predominant virtue; the growth of pluralism merely confirms this. This is why I find it odd that many evangelicals today are surprised about the pluralism and relativism associated with postmodernism. Postmodernism is really not "post" at all; it is merely the full flower of modernism. The autonomy of the individual and the rejection of authority predominant in modernism find their logical conclusion in the pluralism of today. More to the point of our study, this is why the public nature of God's glory is so critical a point to make in our churches today. Pluralism (i.e., freedom) can only thrive when belief is reduced to a private matter. I say this not to cause churches to initiate some plan to enforce Biblical doctrine as the moral code of society. Instead, I am simply pointing out the need to recover a public fortitude to say that beliefs are right or wrong based on the Word of God. Christianity has been silenced, in part, by its commitment to religious freedom. In other words, in order to maintain the freedom of speech we enjoy, we have agreed not to make too much of a nuisance of ourselves in the public square. Even when we do venture into politics, it's on the basis of the "common good" for all society and not some notion of the supremacy of God's revelation. We have not lost our Christian heritage; we have gained a virtue we believe is greater than any revealed doctrine: personal freedom.

Jefferson himself held to a very strong personal sense of privacy regarding religion. Further, he believed religion should remain a matter of individual conscience and not be subjected to concerted public efforts toward unification.

> Early in his studies of society, Jefferson came to the conclusion that religion was essentially an inner and private matter between "every man and his Maker" in which no outside agency, not even the church and certainly not the government, should interfere. He was therefore, he wrote, "most scrupulously reserved on the subject." He went so far as to believe one should not try "to change another's

creed." So he opposed sending missionaries "to make converts" and distributing Bibles outside of America.[6]

Jefferson believed strongly that only the individual conscience was to be trusted in securing appropriate belief for an individual. The state or church may well be equipped to provide excellent input, but any belief, in order to qualify as a belief, must stem from within. Jefferson was convinced the right to individual preference was so sacred that the right must be defended per se, apart from any specific religious belief or doctrine. It is inherent in being human to have the right to choose freely any and all religious conviction, or the lack thereof.

> Freedom of conscience was one of the most important of the rights of man, Jefferson believed, and he was one of the most influential of the American founding fathers in establishing religious freedom as the law of the land. The right to hold varied personal opinions, especially about religion, needed to be defended constantly, even against the "tyranny of public opinion." If necessary, the right to "choose error" must be protected.[7]

Jefferson wanted religion to be only as public as its adherents wished, which for him personally was not at all. His own beliefs and religious convictions were "known to my God and myself alone."[8] By no means does this mean that Jefferson opposed public discussion of religion and its qualities altogether. However, even in public discourse, adherence to religious doctrine must be based in a *reasonable* conviction.[9] The basic presumption of all the founders was, at the very least, a lowest common denominator of religious moral influence on society. Christian and deist alike believed the moral principles of religion could be instantiated

---

6. Charles B. Sanford, *The Religious Life of Thomas Jefferson* (Charlottesville: University Press of Virginia, 1984) 13. Sanford is here quoting Jefferson's correspondence with, in order, Richard Rush, May 31, 1813 (*Writings of Thomas Jefferson*, Ford, 9:385), Mrs. Samuel Harrison Smith, August 6, 1816, and Samuel Greenhow, January 31, 1814 (*The Writings of Thomas Jefferson*, Definitive Edition, ed. by Albert Ellery Bergh, 20 vols. [Washington, DC, 1907] 15:60, 14:81).

7. Sanford, *The Religious Life*, 13. Sanford is quoting Jefferson's correspondence to Edward Dowse, April 19, 1803 (*Writings of Thomas Jefferson*, Bergh, 10:378).

8. Thomas Jefferson correspondence to Matthew Carey, November 11, 1816 (*Writings of Thomas Jefferson*, Ford, 10:67–68).

9. On this, Jefferson and Madison were quite adamant. Jefferson believed a free marketplace of religious ideas would be self-regulating due to a sense of reason shared by all. Thus, religious freedom was the highest ideal and could be sought without compromise of a moral society. See Lambert, *The Founding Fathers*, 227–32.

into the moral life of the new country without compromising individual liberty of conscience. Most of the religious influence would come through churches and the free and reasonable expression of their beliefs and practices. Thus, protection of that freedom was critical to the moral growth of the nation. However, the state also assumed a certain amount of divine activity in establishing the moral life of the settlers and colonists. Humans were, after all, created beings, and their creation entailed a nature and inherent rights. These were theological/anthropological foundations on which all could agree and to which all could sign their name.[10]

The need for public morality combined with a religious climate of individualism created a need for language that would draw together conservative Protestants, seculars more swayed by Enlightenment influences, and all those in between. Divine language remained a part of the daily political discourse on many subjects. Indeed, even secular Enlightenment influences still used the language of God and creation, however they may have believed such things occurred. Nevertheless, sufficient warrant existed for more decidedly sectarian language to be excluded from public documents. Thus, God may be invoked as creator and sustainer of human history. Further, God is even credited with endowing humans with certain "rights" in the Declaration of Independence. However, the founders were careful not to go beyond this into more exclusive claims of Jesus's divine status or power over nature. Certainly some favored such inclusion and others opposed it.[11] The middle ground agreeable to all was a more expedient use of generic "god" language to establish an anthropology rooted in individual autonomy and the reliability of human reason. In the end, no state religion was established, not even the majority voice of Christianity, but the divine lore common to the day was invoked for the sake of sanctioning Enlightenment views of human nature, authenticating the authority of individual conscience in language that was quickly to become law. As the law stands to this day, the conscience now relegates all religious conviction to choice or preference, causing most today to con-

10. For example, the belief that all humans deserved certain unalienable rights given to them by God was as much a theological belief as it was a political belief. Even today, much theological justification is spent on establishing specific political beliefs associated with a Western democracy or with capitalism.

11. E.g., note the debates by John Winthrop, William Williams, and some Puritans of Massachusetts with other founders surrounding the language of the Constitution and its lack of a religious test for officeholders. Cf. Lambert's outline of the necessity for a free religious marketplace in *Founding Fathers*, 236–64.

sider religion *merely* a matter of opinion; and as opinion, it is best kept to the confines of personal thoughts and meditations.[12]

The founders' urge to translate language that was specifically Christian (i.e., Scripture) into more general moral language "for the sake of a more perfect Union" has shown up in various contemporary religious movements. The Social Gospel was an attempt to find moral value socially in the otherwise useless existence of the liberal church. Doctrinal affirmations of the church and statements of belief were merely language that had a regulatory effect on the social practice of the church. Historical criticism gutted belief in the reality of Christian doctrine. Therefore, the value of the language of doctrine was reduced to its sociological influence. In order to avoid losing all meaning whatsoever in the existence of the church, the Social Gospel movement attempted to give primary place to the moral influence of the church on society through acts of benevolence and reform. Thus, Christianity was reduced to its contribution to the "common good." The value of religious belief was finally measured by its effect on the betterment of society. In other words, theology was reduced to sociology. Walter Rauschenbusch (1861–1918), one of the founders of the Social Gospel movement, viewed Christian language as a means to unite all humanity under the collective conscience of a rational moral sense common to all people. Christianity and its language simply represented the best in humanity's struggle to progress in its moral evolution, especially in its social development. "Christianizing means humanizing in the highest sense."[13]

Today, in a similar fashion, we see pluralism subsuming belief under the banner of social welfare. In an attempt to tame any claims to exclusivity or singularity of truth, pluralists reduce Christianity to one of several movements intended to accomplish social improvement. As one pluralist makes clear, "[E]verything that Christians do and say should be governed by concern for justice, freedom, and grace, and never any one of these without the others."[14] The reach of such influences can be seen in the

12. It is the politics of preference, or choice, that has reduced Christian discipleship to merely the presentation of options and wisdom. While certainly these are useful tools for training the moral sensitivities of believers, they are a woeful comparison to the kind of training offered by the discipleship of the New Testament. Thus is the extent of Gnosticism in American Christianity.

13. Walter Rauschenbusch, *Christianizing the Social Order*, (New York: Macmillan, 1919) 125. Rauschenbusch was by no means original in this, since it can be traced back, at least, to Kant's efforts in *Religion within the Limits of Reason Alone* (1793).

14. Tom F. Driver, "The Case for Pluralism," *The Myth of Christian Uniqueness: Toward*

Christian compulsion to translate. Christians are compelled to translate their Christian language into a more secular version in order to appeal to all and avoid the exclusivity of peculiarly Christian claims or terminology. Thus, in the name of pluralism, liberals are led to reduce Christian language to its social implications. Likewise, some conservatives are led to promote the teachings of Christianity under the guise of "family values" or "traditional values." In the name of having greater impact or influence on society, Christians are following the path of reductionism, reducing the language of exclusivity and conversion to the language of inclusion and social welfare. In one sense, the desire to be socially relevant is certainly laudable. It is a public expression of belief in contrast to the compulsion toward the privatization of religion. Such a push for relevance is a determined effort to find a public voice for Christian witness and avoid the Gnostic implications of internalizing belief, which reduces it to the preferences of conscience. However, the tendency to reduce Christianity merely to its social benefit is precisely the downfall of liberalism.[15]

This movement toward reductionism by translating Christianity into more secular language simply illustrates the taboo nature of specifically Christian language in contemporary politics of religion. Generic terms like God and spirituality are acceptable, but anything specific to Jesus or the Gospel is quickly shouted down as exclusive, and therefore, outside the bounds of civil religious discourse. The drive toward privatization should be clear in such a context. Evangelism and public praise are often regarded as risky and may even be restricted in certain public places. In

---

a Pluralistic Theology of Religions, ed. by John Hick and Paul F. Knitter (Maryknoll, NY: Orbis, 1987) 217.

15. The "common good" of all society has always been a political goal for the Christian left, but has seen a surge of support in recent decades by conservative Christians. The commitment to social improvement ranges from pop-theology approaches (e.g., Tom Minnery, *Why You Can't Stay Silent* [Wheaton, IL: Tyndale, 2001]) to more scholarly attempts to justify a common moral ethic for all humanity (e.g., Stephen Charles Mott, *Biblical Ethics and Social Change* [New York: Oxford University Press, 1982]). Along the same lines, Clarke D. Forsythe (*Politics for the Greatest Good: The Case for Prudence in the Public Square*, [Downers Grove, IL: InterVarsity, 2009]) argues for the (Christian?) virtue of prudence in accomplishing the greatest good possible, in slight contrast to the common good. Nevertheless, Forsythe remains committed to the fundamental welfare of society in a manner similar to those Christians advocating a social strategy for the common good of all humanity. The net effect of such a position is to reduce Christianity to just one more sociological scheme intended for the betterment or preservation of all humankind.

such a context, witness becomes a mode of communication, rather than an existence. It's acceptable to believe whatever you want to believe, but you must finally keep it to yourself. How should Christians who regard the Gospel as the supreme reality act in a world that will not accept such a claim as politically valid? The question of the reality of claims such as resurrection, sin, and atonement, rarely raise the ire of people as much as someone speaking of such issues in public. Is "going public" really all that important to Christianity? Is the only reason to "go public" to influence the direction of society?

"LET YOUR LIGHT SHINE BEFORE MEN . . ."

Amidst the voices advocating silence in public settings and keeping belief to one's self, the Scripture seems to compel its adherents to a different posture. Christians are called to "shout for joy from the tops of the mountains" (Isa 42:11). This is not a call for translation of Christian language into the lowest common denominator language of secular morality or party politics. Nor is it a voice of reason common to all humanity in the language of natural law or natural theology. This is the language of praise spoken unashamedly and unreservedly in the presence of believer and unbeliever alike. The history of God's work in and through His people is a history of a very public process of making known His own renown (Isa 26:8). What we mean by public is the work of God performed by the people of God for the purpose of drawing the attention of all creation to the reputation of God. A few familiar illustrations of major movements by God in history should suffice to demonstrate God's public purposes.

After the prologue of Genesis 1–11, the detailed story of God calling His people begins with Abram. God covenants with Abram to make his name great (Gen 12:2) and through him to bless "all the families of the earth" (12:3). God's plan to work through Abram included a public work of blessing that extended beyond Abram and his relatives. Likewise, though God promised Abram and his descendants a land in which to dwell in safety and plentiful provision, God also extends His work amongst His people to a work that includes all nations (Gen 17:16; Deut 15:6; Ps 96).

His work amongst the Jews was intended to make the Jews a unique people, even a holy, or set apart, people. The Mosaic Law was intended to accomplish this, though its limitations are clear (Gal 3). "You shall be holy, for I am holy" (Lev 11:44; 19:2; 20:7) was God's way of declaring the distinct characteristic of His people worshiping the one true and living God. God enacted through the Law and through ethnic identity a calling that made His people distinct, even separate, from all others (Isa 52:11; 2 Cor 6:17). This distinction as God's chosen people was intended to draw the attention of all peoples. As the Lord declares,

> It is too small a thing that You should be My Servant,
>   To raise up the tribes of Jacob and to restore the preserved ones of Israel;
> I will also make You a light of the nations,
>   So that My salvation may reach to the end of the earth. (Isa 49:6)

God did not mean for His name to be known only amongst the Jews alone. Indeed, He wished the nations to know His great works and His salvation.

The reason God is concerned with the nations is not because He is egalitarian in the love He lavishes through salvation, though certainly it is true that He does not wish "for any to perish" (2 Pet 3:9). All too often, an anthropocentric focus seems to limit the scope of God's work to merely a Gospel for humanity. We seem to have lost sight of the more pressing reason for the public nature of God's work: His own glory.

> [22] "Therefore say to the house of Israel, 'Thus says the Lord GOD, "It is not for your sake, O house of Israel, that I am about to act, but for My holy name, which you have profaned among the nations where you went. [23] I will vindicate the holiness of My great name which has been profaned among the nations, which you have profaned in their midst. Then the nations will know that I am the LORD," declares the Lord GOD, "when I prove Myself holy among you in their sight. [24] For I will take you from the nations, gather you from all the lands and bring you into your own land. [25] Then I will sprinkle clean water on you, and you will be clean; I will cleanse you from all your filthiness and from all your idols. [26] Moreover, I will give you a new heart and put a new spirit within you; and I will remove the heart of stone from your flesh and give you a heart of flesh. [27] I will put My Spirit within you and cause you to walk in My statutes, and you will be careful to observe My ordinances. [28] You will live in the land that I gave to your forefathers; so you will be My people, and I will be your God." (Ezek 36:22–28)

If These Become Silent, the Rocks Will Cry Out

God wishes for His reputation to be exalted above any and all other gods of the nations. Notice that this language in Ezekiel is specific to Israel in its promise of land and God's activity to make His people holy. However, this passage is a further expression of God's work in His Christian people of the New Covenant (cf. Jer 31:31–34; Joel 2:28–32; Heb 8:7–13; Acts 2:16–21). The intent of the passage is to show how God will vindicate His reputation by effecting His work of righteousness in His people. He will do this through the means of the Holy Spirit and by renewing the heart. However, more importantly, He will do this *because* He wishes to restore His reputation amongst the nations. His primary concern is His own glory, His own fame, not primarily our welfare. God used the people of Israel to draw attention to Himself. Further, He is using Christians to make His glory known in the world today.

> [W]ork out your salvation with fear and trembling, for it is God who is at work in you, both to will and to work for His good pleasure. Do all things without grumbling or disputing; that you prove yourselves blameless and innocent, children of God above reproach in the midst of a crooked and perverse generation, among whom you appear as lights in the world. (Phil 2:12–15)

God is using His people to make His name known amongst the nations. This is God's public mission: the public restoration of His own reputation.

This may be the best place for mentioning why Scripture remains the primary source for Christians and why inerrancy is still a critical doctrine. In order to know the character of God and have the ability to imitate it, we must have a reliable source. Though it is certainly true that Christians have the Holy Spirit and have a robust tradition of discipleship from which to draw, the only way to know the reliability of which spirit is influencing us and which tradition is to be followed is to finally "read" them alongside our reading of Scripture. In order to be the kind of people who are capable of restoring the reputation of the King of the universe, we must be able to articulate a consistent rendering of His character and message. Only revelational knowledge (i.e., the universal or absolute truth of revelation) can fit this bill.

It may sound like a very arrogant plan God is bringing about through His people: using them to restore His own reputation. However, how could we expect anything else? If a person wished for attention, we would call it pride. For God to demand such attention is simply His recognition of who He is. He is the God of the universe; He made the universe. "I am the LORD your God . . . you shall have no other gods before Me . . . for I the LORD your God am a jealous God" (Exod 20:2, 3, 5). For anyone or anything to garner more fame or attention than Him would be idolatry.

THE CROSS ON CENTER STAGE

The Incarnation of Jesus is one of the more profound events of human history. Here we have the Lord of the universe, the One by whom and for whom all things were made (Col 1:16), humbling Himself to take on the likeness of His own creatures. In so doing, He embraces a limitation of His own rights to divine power, while at the same time not compromising His divine status. In other words, He "emptied Himself" (Phil 2:7). I cannot fathom an analogy that would display the profound depths of this event. It was announced publicly by the angels at Jesus's birth (Luke 2:8–14) and seems to have remained a subject of public conversation throughout Jesus's earthly life (note the derogatory comment on Jesus's origin in John 8:41). The Word becoming flesh is a miracle due constant meditation and awe. However, this is only the beginning of the story. In Jesus's birth as a human, God is setting the stage for an even greater event, demanding more than mere attention; the cross demands worship.

The spectacle of the cross is somewhat baffling. Is this really God's success story? The cross seems like failure; it seems like the final resignation of a vanquished hero—no friends, no defenders, no second chances. The cross was the height of public humiliation. Why would this event be the event of the ages? Why would God wish to display publicly what seems like defeat? The answers to these questions are ancient, yet renewed each day in their confirmation.

Sin wishes to remain a secret. In fact, people will go to great lengths to hide the truth of their failures. Of course, the Bible makes it clear that sin is not a secret; the light will eventually expose the secrets of our hearts (1 Cor 4:5; Eph 5:11–13). God sees every deed and knows every thought (Ps 139:1–4). Further, it seems as though the Accuser knows of such deeds as well (Rev 12:10). What may seem to be secret on earth is actually very public before God's throne. Sin does not remain hidden before God, and seemingly before His angels as well; we are never without an audience. Public sin demands public atonement. Public shame and guilt demand public restoration. These are the reasons why Jesus must die on the public stage of the cross. But why such a humiliating death?

We have already seen that God's primary concern in creating a holy people is so that all creation might see His own holiness displayed and vindicated. As will be discussed in greater detail in the next chapter, such a display is perhaps best understood in the context of honor and shame.[16] Both honor and shame have a personal connotation as we feel them in our heart and conscience. However, they seem best defined in the public venue of bringing honor or shame to a group or reputation. Shame bears a much greater sting if our sin becomes publicly known. We spend a great deal of time discussing the fact that Jesus bore our guilt on the cross, taking away our debt due to sin. This legal transaction explains well the price Jesus paid for appeasing God's wrath. However, it does little to explain the reason Jesus must die such a humiliating death.

Our public defamation of God's character required public restoration of His reputation. This was true in the OT (e.g., the flood, David and Bathsheba, etc.); it is no less true in the NT. Jesus "humbled Himself by becoming obedient to the point of death, even death on a cross" (Philippians 2:8) so that He might remove the shame associated with God's name due to sin. Humanity was an embarrassment to its creator, though God owed no explanation to anyone. God was not ashamed before a public that judged Him inept or incapable. Instead, God's grief at creating humanity was before Himself (Gen 6:6–7). He was, and is, His own primary audience, and in His own view of His creation after the Fall, humanity was humiliating. This is the definition of shame: the sense of humiliation associated with one's reputation. God's reputation was compromised before a watching audience, which subjected Him to ridicule. But even more importantly, He felt the sting of personal shame in the loss of His created intentions. Of course, the point of Scripture is not the loss, but on what was gained at the cross. In order to restore honor, the stigma of sin's humiliation must be removed. In other words, Jesus's work on the cross not only bought the debt of sinners before God, it also restored honor in God's presence and in the presence of all who watched *by the way He suffered humiliation and death*. Certainly, for Jesus, the God of the universe, the creator of all, suffering pain and anguish at the hands of those He had made was a

---

16. For further development of the themes of honor and shame and their impact on missions, see Roland Muller, *Honor and Shame: Unlocking the Door* (Philadelphia: Xlibris, 2000).

humiliation beyond compare. But an even greater humiliation is observed in the fact that Jesus "gave up His spirit" (John 19:30). He did not have to die; He chose to die (John 10:17–18). His death was a radical departure from the privilege He deserved as creator and the only one worthy to judge. So radical is Jesus's death that it seems almost to be a joke, a satire on the rights to privilege craved by the Devil. It is in the depths of Jesus's lack of obligation that humiliation and shame are born. He didn't have to die, but He wanted it anyway. He chose death that He might restore honor by making a laughingstock of death's right to judgment and accusation.

Jesus's resurrection is all the more triumphant in that it is a celebration of the removal of death's stigma associated with the humiliation of sin. Not only have Christians been legally delivered from the kingdom of darkness and transferred to the kingdom of light (Col 1:13), we also have been set free from the sting of death, gaining victory over its power to shame us (1 Cor 15:54–57). Sin and death are publicly humiliating, which probably explains why people shun conversations on these subjects. But God has always dealt with them "head on." He defeated all claims against those formerly in bondage to sin, "When He had disarmed the rulers and authorities, He made a public display of them, having triumphed over them through Him." (Col 2:15). In the resurrection, God made a public spectacle of the defeated enemies of His triumphant redemption, so that He might place the shame where it belonged. The Law of Moses only revealed our inability to escape sin's mastery over us and its attendant shame. However, the cross makes it clear that Christians are no longer subject to sin as master; we are enslaved to the righteousness of God. We are no longer subject to "the things of which [we] are now ashamed" (Rom 6:21). Instead, we have been set free from the mastery and shame of sin. We are now legitimate heirs, even children of God, and as children, we enjoy the privilege of a relationship free from guilt and the embarrassment of sin (Rom 8:12–17).

Being set free from sin is a personal matter, but it is an even more important public event than we usually imagine it to be. Unfortunately, we don't really grasp the nature of baptism in the West. We have spent so much time debating the magical powers of water and the obligatory nature of baptism, that we have lost sight of perhaps the most potent meaning associated with being lowered into water in front of a crowd. The meaning of baptism becomes clearer in the context of the cross's humiliation. As a person is lowered into the water, the association with

Jesus's death is obvious. However, less obvious is the association with His humility. We are "baptized into His death" (Rom 6:3). This association of believers with the same identity of Christ in His death is an association that extends beyond simply legal terms of identification. Paul is here laying out a path to follow while enjoying life on this earth. It is a path of suffering and shame, though we know that the shame is not permanent. We strive to "know Him and the power of His resurrection and the fellowship of His sufferings, being conformed to His death; in order that I may attain to the resurrection from the dead." (Phil 3:10–11). This is an association that connotes shame; however, the weight of shame is diverted due to the expectation of a life lived in honor and eventual salvation from the dead; it is replaced with an even greater weight of glory in salvation. "For this reason I also suffer these things, *but I am not ashamed*; for I know whom I have believed and I am convinced that He is able to guard what I have entrusted to Him until that day." (2 Tim 1:12 [emphasis mine]; cf. Romans 1:16). Baptism is, rightly, understood as identification with the death and shame of Christ. It is also a celebration of victory over these things, but that victory is postponed until we attain the resurrection. We can grow weary or tire of waiting. That is why Paul encourages us not to grow weary in living for the sake of the Lord's honor (1 Cor 15:58; Gal 6:9; 2 Thess 3:13). We have a hope that is real, secure ... even glorious. Baptism is the public declaration that sin and shame have been conquered through the Lord of glory. We rise from the water in public declaration of Jesus's Lordship over death and its consequences. The primary point of baptism is the public statement it makes about our transformation from enslavement to sin to the Lordship of Jesus—a Lordship that is meant to be seen publicly in our words and actions (1 Pet 3:15–22).

A ROSE BY ANY OTHER NAME

We are all familiar with Shakespeare's love of beauty. He is quite fond of comparing women and their virtue to gardens and flowers. He uses the most beautiful things he can imagine to express what he regards as the fairest comparison to a high-quality display of character. Likewise, he is fond of comparing physical beauty with the intricacies of flowers in their prime. Perhaps Shakespeare was simply recounting an analogy common to humanity's astonishment at creation, or perhaps he was borrowing an analogy already made for him in the pages of Scripture.

Flowers were used by the authors of Scripture to depict great beauty. The bride in the Song of Solomon described herself as "the rose of Sharon, the lily of the valleys" (Song 2:1). The bride is here describing how she has been prepared for her groom and the beauty is not only physical but also virtuous. The groom admires her great beauty and the preparation of her virtue and calls her "my beautiful one" (2:13).

God Himself speaks in "flowery" language when describing the restoration of Israel after her return from idolatry.

> [4] I will heal their apostasy,
> I will love them freely,
> For My anger has turned away from them.
> [5] I will be like the dew to Israel;
> He will blossom like the lily,
> And he will take root like the cedars of Lebanon.
> [6] His shoots will sprout,
> And his beauty will be like the olive tree
> And his fragrance like the cedars of Lebanon.
> [7] Those who live in his shadow
> Will again raise grain,
> And they will blossom like the vine.
> His renown will be like the wine of Lebanon.
> [8] O Ephraim, what more have I to do with idols?
> It is I who answer and look after you.
> I am like a luxuriant cypress;
> From Me comes your fruit.
> [9] Whoever is wise, let him understand these things;
> Whoever is discerning, let him know them.
> For the ways of the LORD are right,
> And the righteous will walk in them,
> But transgressors will stumble in them. (Hos 14:4–9)

God compares the righteousness of Israel, and in verse 9 the righteousness of us, to lilies, cedars, olive trees, the blossoms of the vine, the cypress, etc. He is pointing to the beauty of righteousness by making an analogy of the most beautiful things in creation we can imagine—things meant to be seen and admired. In the context of the above quote from Hosea, such beauty is in stark contrast to the disgrace of Hosea's plight with Gomer. His marriage to a harlot was a public humiliation meant to draw attention to the faithfulness of God in spite of Israel's harlotry. The public restoration envisioned in these verses overshadows all former embarrassment and pain. God's work of restoration will always overshadow the careless creep of sin into the crevices of daily living, as surely as the sun sends shadows scurrying to their deaths.

It is interesting to note that technology is yet to replace the beauty of living blossoms. We are attracted to real flowers and growing green gardens, because they reach beyond the senses into the soul inside us where beauty dwells. God's appreciation of beauty is surely no less than ours. Indeed, He finds our righteousness, our faithful allegiance, so beautiful that flowers are its only comparison. It is hard to imagine that anything could distract us from the beauty of a flower, but God's righteousness displayed for all eyes to see causes even the flower to pale. Jesus picks up on this analogy in Matthew 6 when He points out the way in which God cares for His creation.

> [28] "And why are you worried about clothing? Observe how the lilies of the field grow; they do not toil nor do they spin, [29] yet I say to you that not even Solomon in all his glory clothed himself like one of these. [30] But if God so clothes the grass of the field, which is alive today and tomorrow is thrown into the furnace, will He not much more clothe you? You of little faith! [31] Do not worry then, saying, 'What will we eat?' or 'What will we drink?' or 'What will wear for clothing?' [32] For the Gentiles eagerly seek all these things; for your heavenly Father knows that you need all these things. [33] But seek first His kingdom and His righteousness, and all these things will be added to you." (Matt 6:28–33)

It is pertinent that Jesus should draw attention to the faithfulness of God in His care for His creatures. Further, it does not seem random that Jesus should choose the lily to draw attention to the way in which God provides for the daily needs of clothing. Jesus seems to be introducing an element of beauty into the analogy for the sake of pointing out how beautiful is God's work for humans as well. Further, our faith is a counterpoint in this equation of beauty. Being content in seeking His kingdom alone is the final variable that completes the picture of glory envisioned by Jesus in our relationship to the Father's provision.

The point of all these analogies in the paragraphs above is manifold. The authors obviously wish to express and explain the faithfulness of God in caring for and sanctifying His people. However, we as readers must not miss the point that this process is not merely utilitarian. Instead, it is finally to be seen as a thing of beauty. When God crafts righteousness and holiness in His people, it is a work of art that audiences of the ages are to see as a spectacle of His hand. This beauty is not due to the fact that humans have any inherent attractiveness; rather, it is the beauty of what God has done that is remarkable. God takes people steeped in sin and in love with darkness, and He accomplishes the work to transform them into instruments of worship and praise. The beauty is precisely the story of His work and His glory. All eyes are finally fixed on the One who has done this, for *He is beautiful!* David understood this: "One thing I have asked from the LORD, that I shall seek: That I may dwell in the house of the LORD all the days of my life, to behold the *beauty* of the LORD and to meditate in His temple" (Ps 27:4). This is public beauty that is climactic in drawing glory to the reputation of its architect. Further, we are "partakers of the divine nature" (2 Pet 1:4), participants in God's beauty, as He does a mighty work in us before natural and supernatural audiences, even before His own eyes. God wishes to do His public work of glory in a striking manner by drawing attention to the righteousness of His people—a righteousness caused by His hand and provided only through the power of the cross. Salvation makes our lives and the life of the church "viewable" by God. What a wondrous display!

THE END OF ALL GLORY

It seems to be a common characteristic in human nature to desire understanding. From the toddlers' queries, "Why?" to the scholars' reasoned attempts at explanation, we are drawn to conclusions and the display of cause and effect. One could argue that such curiosity may be stronger in certain eras of history, but humanity is never without a passion to know. We feel incomplete without some explanation, perhaps even a simple one created in our imaginations. Stories of the ages, from ancient pictographs to modern movies, attempt to successfully convey a message – a message narrated with a beginning and an end. Some may be clearer than others, but the pattern remains.

At times, we have all stepped back from personal circumstances and pondered the overarching reasons for what God is doing. The final question for this article is, "What is the overarching reason that lies behind even the sum total of all the personal circumstances experienced throughout all history?" In other words, "What is God's final public goal?"

"What do we see God doing in Scripture that continues today and will culminate in the glory of the eschaton?"

Wolfhart Pannenberg's devotion to history is renowned. Like Karl Barth, Pannenberg believes Christology to be the hub of theology and Jesus to be the pinnacle of revelation.[17] Pannenberg has written extensively on the importance of history and on the way history substantiates God's work in the resurrection.[18] Further, Pannenberg saw a purpose of God that stretched even higher than the resurrection. Though Pannenberg wrote His theology "from below," he saw, unfolded in Scripture, the design of God's plan for the ages: the establishment of the Lordship of Jesus over all creation. In a manner similar to Jürgen Moltmann's conception of hope, Pannenberg conceives of history as a purposeful plan that culminates in the return of Christ to authenticate His kingship that has been true all along, but only manifest now in the church. It's like a story that has a happy ending where the king who endured a concealed existence throughout his early reign is finally revealed to all His subjects as their sovereign. Some may have followed him previously with devotion, but now all must pay homage. His kingship was never in question, but its overarching authority was not always plainly seen in the course of his country's affairs.

Relying on passages such as Phil 1:10–11 and Heb 1:12, Pannenberg has devised what he calls a proleptic understanding of history, where Jesus's Lordship is as true now as it ever has been or ever will be, but it will not be seen in its fullness until He is revealed as King in the end of times.[19] Then, the Lordship that has been true all along in the church will be seen and given its due by all creation. Then, His Lordship, though it suffers no lack in the present, will be fully experienced and authenticated when He returns to the earth in all His glory, honor, power, and authority.[20]

---

17. On these points, I wholeheartedly agree with Barth and Pannenberg. Unfortunately, neither held to a dependability of Scripture that could be called inerrant. To one degree or another, they never quite left certain liberal presuppositions behind in discussing the historical reliability of the texts autographed by eyewitnesses. This forced upon them a sort of canon within the canon when it came to choosing which texts could be used reliably and which could not.

18. E.g., see Wolfhart Pannenberg, *Jesus—God and Man*, trans. by Lewis L. Wilkins and Duane A. Priebe, 2nd ed. (Philadelphia: Westminster, 1968).

19. Wolfhart Pannenberg, *Systematic Theology*, vol. 3, trans. by Geoffrey W. Bromiley (Grand Rapids: Eerdmans, 1998) 37. Cf. Ibid., 45, 47.

20. For a more complete discussion of Pannenberg's support of this notion and its out-

Pannenberg's conception of history lays out for us a way of envisioning God's public purposes. In Trinitarian language, the Son's purpose in His first advent was to glorify the Father through obedience, even obeying to the level of giving His life "as a ransom for many" (Mark 10:45). The Son's purpose in His second advent will be to take His throne and authenticate the authority that is already His "in heaven and on earth" (Matt 28:18). Until then, the Father and Son have sent the Spirit to cause the Son's glory to be revealed in His chosen people (John 16:14). The Father is orchestrating the public glorification of the Son in a slow but very sure movement in history. It is public in the sense that it can be seen in places now and will finally be seen fully in all of creation at the end of time. The publicity the Father wishes for His Son's glory is being slowly developed, though this by no means implies that it is inevitably growing in its scope or attention for its human audience. Scripture does not seem to lay out a definite progression of the kingdom to the point that it is waiting for Jesus upon His return. The focus is not on the creation or the courses of history; it is on the Son. All God's public work in creation points to the Son. Everything God does is public in one respect or another, though we may not grasp the depth of His intentions. Of this we can be certain: God wishes for the church to glorify the Son until He returns to take His rightful place as Lord on David's throne. So powerful is this intention that it permeates even our anthropology: We were created and saved to bring glory to the Son (Eph 2:10). Such high purposes rebuff the anthropocentric gospels of our age. We live for the sake of another, even as the Son lived for the sake of another and not Himself. Like unto angels and saints of old "of whom the world was not worthy" (Heb 11:38), where are the Christians whose existence is testimony to the glory of God?

CONCLUSION

Amidst the voices and forces that push us toward keeping our beliefs to ourselves, we must strive to develop a sense of the self that believes it must praise or die. Such a conception of our existence implies a mission for the church that is very different from mere survival until the Son's return. Nor is it our goal to make our nest here on earth more comfortable or prosperous. Instead, we thrive in the ambitions of a kingdom that is not our own.

---

working in the church in Trinitarian terms, see Gale Heide, *System and Story: Narrative Critique and Construction in Theology* (Eugene, OR: Pickwick, 2009) 85–88.

If These Become Silent, the Rocks Will Cry Out

We are the spectacle of history, in that we are the tools of public glory crafted and moved by God for the sake of His own reputation. The world's attempts at domesticating the church into privatized belief have been all too successful. Our language has been translated into the language of "common good." Unwittingly, we have made a contract with the world for a sense of place that doesn't infringe on anyone else's beliefs, so long as they don't infringe on ours. Perhaps, the world will take a drastic step toward disrupting this relationship. We may see the end of certain rights in our generation. What will be the consequences for the church and God's reputation? Our prayer is, as always, "O may Your glorious name be blessed and exalted above all blessing and praise!" (Neh 9:5)—"to Him be the glory in the church and in Christ Jesus to all generations forever and ever. Amen!" (Eph 3:21).

FIVE

The Earth Is My Footstool

The Universal Politics of God's Honor!

AT THIS POINT IN our discussion, it may seem as though my critical remarks are simply so much complaining about personal dissatisfaction with America and the Enlightenment foundations of Western culture. Any criticism of America seems like the liberal pleading of peace protesters who feel ashamed of the evil that we, as humans, are capable of displaying. (Of course, those who study Scripture know that we should not be surprised by human sinfulness.) However, the criticism I am leveling is not aimed at the events of current history, nor are they whines of discontentment so easily dismissed by the "America—Love It or Leave It" crowd. Instead, they are meant to question the very foundation on which America is built, or better, the foundation on which evangelical Christianity has built its support for the ideology underlying American politics.

It is quite certain that America makes being a Christian easier and safer than other countries. The promise of freedom expressed in freedom of religion and freedom of speech allows the church to carry on its business without interruption or fear. These are assets to the church that are, rightly, appreciated. At the same time, we should not simply turn a blind eye to the ways in which such freedoms adversely affect the church. First, it should be noted that freedom is not always free. I don't mean by this that people fight and die to preserve the political ideologies of America, though certainly they do. Dying in battle is but one expression of the ways in which freedom is not really all that free. What is more interesting about American freedom is that, while it holds out the promise of self-determination and personal autonomy, in fact, it simply camouflages the state's control until such a time as the state requires something of its people.

The ownership the state claims on its citizens can be kept out of sight for most of the time. However, each time we speak the Pledge of Allegiance or show respect to the flag as it presides over various events, we are reminded that the state is aware of its own power and is ready and capable of asserting its authority. This is a situation under which the church can thrive, as long as we remain aware of the fact that we are not truly free. On occasion the church has come to believe it has more power than it really does. In other words, we have on occasion become enamored with influence or control; such that we believe a certain amount of freedom is necessary to ground our existence as church. The ideology of political freedom and the allure of personal freedom, though not necessarily incompatible with the function of the church, have made being the church all too easy, and yet at the same time, very difficult.

Of course, the church has been aware of its lack of freedom since its inception. Certainly, levels of state control over the church have been a constant reminder throughout the centuries of how the church exists under human authorities. State authorities have exercised varying levels of ownership over the church and its members, claiming the right to take not only their freedoms and finances, but their very lives as well. Americans seem to live with a sleeping giant of authority who is only occasionally aroused. At the same time, the church has always been confronted by God's authority over her direction and functions. While not nearly as visible as the state, God has far more permeating and comprehensive authority over the church. American freedom has occasionally coerced us into believing we maintain some level of control over human destiny, but Scripture constantly reminds us that our own actions are under the rule and direction of the Almighty. Even further, our very existence is purposed for His glory, which is finally our glory as well.

To this point in our study, we have focused mainly on human politics, that is, how humans interact with one another, relate to authority, and establish consensus. In this chapter, we will dedicate more attention to the politics of God. To be more specific, we will attempt to understand the politics of our relationship with God and how He wishes to exert His power and authority over all of His creation. This is politics with eternal import, since we are no longer trying to sort out what is merely a good way to survive or get along in the world. Instead, we will attend to the universal Lordship of our King. His Lordship commands all creation for all of time. We cannot get any more political than that.

THE HONOR OF GLORY

In most Western cultures, the predominant paradigm for understanding ethics is "right or wrong." Something is "right" when it conforms to the standard established by law or custom; something is "wrong" when it breaks the laws or customs. This makes ethical behavior relatively clear, though by no means easy, since the laws usually spell out what is normative. When applied to Scripture, obedience is the path to sanctification and growth in holiness, since a person is conforming to and embracing what is "right" in the eyes of God. Certainly gray areas exist that keep the discussion of ethics interesting, but the focus remains centered on what is right or wrong, what is legal or illegal.

Unfortunately, such an approach to holiness seems rather minimalistic. In other words, obedience aims at the lowest common denominator. Surely, we may attempt to overcome this by compelling Christians to do not only what is right, but also do it with the right attitude and for the right reasons. In this way we are attempting to engage both heart and action in obedience. However, the end or goal (the telos) of the action and attitude is still centered on the individual engaged in the action. The crux of obedience is the performance of the action, which typically limits the meaning of the action to itself. Obedience is promoted for its own sake and the action carries significance in itself. As will be discussed later in this chapter, some have attempted to move beyond this by exploring the "why" of doing the action (for the glory of God and our greatest pleasure), and in so doing have introduced some extremely beneficial paradigms for understanding and evaluating human action. However, the West still seems unable to fully comprehend how personal holiness matters to God, let alone brings honor to His name, since holiness has more to do with character than it does the simple doing of what is "right or wrong." Some help may be gained by insights from Eastern culture, which is of course, the culture from which much of the Scripture originates.

Roland Muller has given us wonderful help in identifying where West meets East and how the West could gain insight into Scripture from an understanding of Eastern culture, especially Arab culture. His work, *Honor and Shame*, is a brief discussion of how these notions function in the East. Muller lays out three primary worldviews as he views the cultures of the world: guilt—innocence; shame—honor; and fear—power.[1]

---

1. Roland Muller, *Honor and Shame*, 19–20.

The Earth Is My Footstool

As will be discussed, the concepts of honor and shame stand in marked contrast to the Western notions of "right and wrong."

The fear—power model is his attempt to encapsulate the way in which various cultures have identified the movements of nature and people, representing each movement by a supernatural power. Spirits are at work and are the primary means by which any activity may be understood or construed. Humans are subject to these spirits and must either appease or bless them in ways that will afford humanity the most beneficent attitudes and actions from the spirits. Though sometimes viewed as culturally primitive, this worldview is extremely persuasive to those within it and seems closely linked to much of the discussion in Scripture regarding the supernatural encounters of Jesus and others with the demonic world.

The more interesting discussion for our purposes is the difference between the guilt—innocence model and the shame—honor model. Though all three models function at some level in all cultures, one is often most predominant. Muller makes it clear how the guilt—innocence model functions primarily in the West and the shame—honor model functions primarily in Eastern cultures. Those of us from American culture can easily resonate with the guilt—innocence model.

> Almost every major issue the west struggles with involves an aspect of deciding whether something is right or wrong. We arrive at this basic tension in life because almost everything in our culture is plotted between guilt and innocence. (Innocence being something we define as being right or righteousness.)[2]

Muller goes on to explain how guilt and innocence drive much of human activity in the West. This mindset has become so ingrained in the Western conscience that the response to guilt, or at least our avoidance of it comes as second nature. We even go to great lengths to avoid feelings of guilt. "In order not to point our finger at people, we continue to expand the limits of what is acceptable activity. By making homosexuality acceptable, we help thousands of people avoid feeling guilty."[3] Perhaps this avoidance is due to the influence of modern psychology on Western culture.[4] Or perhaps it is due to the way in which Christianity has influenced Western culture. When the Bible and the guilt—innocence model collide, a certain

---

2. Ibid., 23.
3. Ibid., 25.
4. Ibid., 23, 52.

paradigm of legal interpretation often arises, though this is not necessarily the same thing as legalism. Further, an atmosphere of guilt typically accompanies a legal interpretation of Christianity.

Perhaps the best place to observe the way in which the guilt—innocence model has influenced biblical interpretation is in the way Americans typically share the Gospel.

"When trying to share the gospel in our western culture, we usually start from the premise of guilt, as taught in Romans 3. All are guilty of breaking God's law."[5] Muller points out that two of the more popular methods for sharing the Gospel are legal scenarios in which guilt of the person due to permeating sinfulness and God's pardon through Christ's sacrifice are the primary points of the message.[6] This does not make the message wrong or skewed, being highly influenced by legal terminology (e.g., justification). Indeed, the Bible uses such terminology and concepts to explain the Gospel. However, this is not the only paradigm in which the Gospel is portrayed. The language of Scripture seems to lend itself to many cultural paradigms.

Eastern culture seems built upon an entirely different model of thought and action, especially when it comes to moral behavior. Training in this, as in any, worldview begins in childhood.

> As parents, we teach our children to act rightly. If they don't, we teach them feelings of guilt are the proper response. In a shame-based culture, children are taught to act honorably, and if they don't, feelings of shame are the proper response.[7]

The difference between feelings of guilt and feelings of shame are best defined in the context of relationship. Since Western culture is premised on the primacy of the individual, guilt is a personal emotion or sense of remorse/regret. Though others may sympathize, or even empathize, with the guilty party's remorse, the guilt is bore by the guilty individual alone. Eastern culture, premised as it is on the group (e.g., a tribe) grounds its morality in the social network of the community. "In order for shame-based cultures to work, shame and honor are usually attached to some-

---

5. Ibid., 24.

6. Ibid., 36–38. Muller points to the "Romans Road" and the "Four Spiritual Laws" as models of guilt—innocence Gospel presentations. Here he is not arguing that these models are incorrect, only that they are very Western in nature and perception.

7. Ibid., 48.

thing greater than the individual. Honor is almost always placed on a group."[8] Shame is therefore a blight on far more than the individual's conscience, "self-esteem," or reputation. Instead, it is a cloud over the entire group. The reputation of the group can be compromised by the acts of an individual. On the other hand, honor created by the individual reflects well on the entire group.

Of course, such communal ethics means that remedying shame is the responsibility of the group as well. The first response to a shameful act is to attempt to cover it up.[9] If a shameful act becomes known, it must then be revenged.[10] It is the stories of revenge, or reclaiming honor for the group, that make the headlines. We have all read stories of older brothers or fathers in Arab countries killing their own sisters or daughters because of the shame they brought on the family due to some indiscretion or perceived indiscretion. Even in Western history, putting criminals in stocks and marking criminals or adulteresses was a means for publicly shaming those who violated the accepted codes of conduct. The difference, of course, is that Western shame was typically isolated to the individual, and Eastern shame is shared by the entire group.

Honor is similar to shame with respect to the relationship of the individual to the community. The reputation of the group takes precedence over the individual to such an extent that even the personal welfare of the individual may become expendable if the honor of the group is in question. Personal desires and the "right" to pursue one's own happiness are subjected to what is best for the group. It is honorable to pursue activities that will raise the moral reputation of the group. Further, it is honorable to avoid shame or to take responsibility for shameful deeds. In such a context, suicide for the sake of the group's reputation and welfare is understood as an act of high moral good. Muller relates the story of Asian students committing suicide because they received poor grades in their coursework at school.[11] Such an interpretation of suicide does not necessarily overcome the problematic nature of taking one's own life. It simply points out the level of commitment existing in other cultures to the honor of the group. The individual is seen primarily as an extension

---

8. Ibid., 50.
9. Ibid., 81–82.
10. Ibid., 85–86.
11. Ibid., 49–50.

of the group. Therefore, life is lived for the sake of another, or even the reputation of another, rather than for self. This concept will become more pertinent below when we begin to discuss how God's honor might take precedence over individual desires.

Understanding this paradigm can have momentous affects on sharing the Gospel in Eastern or other similar cultures. Certainly, humanity is in a position of guilt, due to its state of sinfulness (Rom 3:23). And certainly justification comes through Jesus (Rom 3:24). However, an aspect of the Gospel that is sometimes overlooked or misunderstood by Western theologians is the shame associated with humanity's sinfulness and the honor that comes through salvation in Christ. Muller points to passages like Lev 26:13 and 1 Pet 2:6.

> I am the LORD your God, who brought you out of the land of Egypt so that you should not be their slaves, and I broke the bars of your yoke and made you walk erect (or upright). (Lev 26:13)
> Behold I lay in Zion a choice stone, a precious corner stone, And he who believes in Him shall not be put to shame.
> (1 Pet 2:6)

These and other passages indicate that the children of the Lord experience shame due to their position as outcasts from the presence of God, and they are honored when the Lord brings them near through salvation. Indeed, as Muller points out by rehearsing some of the clear salvation analogies in Scripture, God will raise believers up to a position of honor as joint heirs with Christ.[12] Such a paradigm shift in sharing the Gospel does not exclude other paradigms as appropriate means for understanding and explaining the Gospel, such as the guilt—innocence model. In fact, any of the three models of culture, and the related strategies for sharing the Gospel, may be useful in any of the other cultural contexts. They are by no means mutually exclusive; rather, they are quite complementary. Consequently, the task in sharing the Gospel in various cultural contexts is to discern, rather than presume cultural influences and biases.

---

12. Muller, *Honor and Shame*, 59–66. Here Muller outlines the biblical notions of God moving believers from a position of defiled to cleansed, from naked to clothed, from expelled (from Eden and God's presence) to being brought near by God, etc., to demonstrate that shame is a central theme in Scripture from which God is established as the Savior. Further, the removal of shame is typically accompanied by a magnificent gesture of God's grace, such as cleansing or clothing those formerly ashamed (e.g., Adam and Eve in the garden). Such honor does not diminish God's honor, but magnifies it as we share in it.

Our discussion thus far has focused on the specifics of each cultural model or paradigm. The purpose of outlining these models is to open up further means to understand how honor functions in Scripture. We have seen that honor is something God grants to those He saves. However, we have yet to understand the purpose and place of how humans may pursue honor in the biblical story. By this, I do not mean personal honor, for it is unseemly to raise yourself to a place of honor in the Eastern culture. Likewise, Scripture advocates humility before God and others, allowing honor to be bestowed, rather than obtained.

> Jesus makes it plain in the Sermon on the Mount that God honors the humble, not the proud. If God honors the proud, they only get more proud. But when the humbled are honored, they simply grow more humble and return the honor onto the one honoring them.[13]

Instead of seeking our own honor, I wish to discuss how we might bring honor to Jesus through His body, the church. For this we will begin by turning to the good work of John Piper.

THE DESIRE OF NATIONS,

or The Consuming Happiness of Knowing God

For many years now, Piper has concentrated his writing and speaking efforts on heralding the supremacy of God. His earlier works, *Desiring God* and *The Pleasures of God* were an attempt to help Christians realize the permeating nature of God's glory. Piper has continued a prolific writing campaign to draw attention to the fact that all of human existence is designed to amplify the honor and glory of God's name, or reputation. The magnification of God's honor is the supreme purpose for all created history.

God is first and foremost concerned with His own reputation and the enjoyment He finds in Himself. To attribute such preoccupation with the self to people would be arrogance. However, for God to be so concerned with His reputation is merely an affirmation that He is God. As mentioned earlier in the Introduction, Piper revises the Westminster Confession slightly to reflect this preoccupation: "The chief end of *God* is

---

13. Muller, *Honor and Shame*, 67.

to glorify God and enjoy himself forever."[14] Granting primacy to anything other than Himself would be idolatry for God.

A unique implication of such an understanding for human existence is that it rightly grants humans a derived value. In other words, God's purposes are supreme, and humans are a means to that end, not ends in themselves (contra Immanuel Kant). Piper continues to encourage human welfare by demonstrating that true joy is discovered when humans delight in God.

> [T]he faith which pleases God is the assurance that when we turn to him we will find the All-satisfying Treasure. We will find our heart's eternal delight. But do you see what this implies? It implies that something has happened in our hearts *before* the act of faith. It implies that beneath and behind the act of faith which pleases God, a new taste has been created. A taste for the glory of God and the beauty of Christ. Behold, a joy has been born![15]

However, human happiness is not the final end of delighting in God. Piper believes that God's greatest purpose is to bring honor and glory to Himself, *and* the greatest joy of humanity is to fulfill our created purpose to live, think, and feel in such a way as to accomplish His glory (Isa 43:7). The two notions are not necessarily antithetical; they are simultaneous and symbiotic. Thus, Piper finds himself compelling humans to strive after the greatest happiness they can possibly discover: the fulfillment of their destiny to honor God's reputation. Again revising the Westminster Confession slightly, Piper concludes "The chief end of man is to glorify God BY enjoying him forever."[16] Christian hedonism is the name Piper uses to describe this agenda, but any more sophisticated theological study of the Scriptures would lead to the same conclusion: Human happiness is discovered in God's glory.[17]

14. John Piper, *Desiring God: Meditations of a Christian Hedonist* (Portland, OR: Multnomah, 1986) 23.

15. Ibid., 53. Emphasis his.

16. Ibid., 14.

17. Piper's *Desiring God* is dedicated to expounding on a development and defense of Christian hedonism. Though the word "hedonist" may conjure some rather un-Christian notions, Piper does an admirable job of exploring the notion along Aristotelian lines that human purposes appropriately center on the pursuit of happiness. His challenge is not to abandon the primacy of human life as a means to God's ends. On the contrary, he wishes to equivocate between human happiness and the pursuit of God's glory. His challenge is to those who would promote a Spartan lifestyle as the only means appropriate to secure God's honor.

Though Piper never seems to draw the conclusion, his work has political implications. He has carefully and correctly laid out the purpose of human existence, in so far as Scripture describes it. In so doing, he has denied the autonomy of the individual by making humans a means to a greater end than themselves. One may wish to argue that by pursuing happiness in God, the Christian hedonist is still acting out of selfish motives, thereby sustaining the individual as politically foundational. However, Piper answers such an objection directly.

> We are commanded by the Word of God, "Delight yourself in the LORD." This means: Pursue joy in God. The word "joy" or "delight" protects us from a mercenary pursuit of God. And the phrase "in God" protects us from thinking joy somehow stands alone as an experience separate from our experience of God himself.[18]

No one can say he or she has found fulfillment apart from finding pleasure in knowing God. In other words, God and His greatness are *a priori* to the experience of Him, making the experience a derived encounter. We do experience the pleasure of knowing God as a reality, but only in so far as the self is consumed by the presence of His glory, or better, unified to His glorious presence. This is by no means a divinizing of humanity, as if we should be raised to the level of God. It is, however, a true union with the Triune Godhead as we attempt to assume Christlikeness in the way He existed to honor the Father. Christ's greatest joy was to honor the Father's will. Our greatest pleasure is to walk in His steps through the daily cares of life. This is not selfish pleasure. Indeed, it is selfless pleasure.

THE RECIPROCATING HONOR OF GOD

Theologically speaking, living for the honor of Jesus means believers are called to live in such a way as to demonstrate His righteousness. "Let your light so shine before men that they may see your good works and give glory (honor) to your Father who is in heaven" (Matt 5:16). Honoring the Father comes through living a life that demonstrates His honor in human action. Of course, the natural question is, "Which actions?" In other words, "How will we know our actions bring Him honor?" The answer is quite simple, though altogether difficult as well. It is discovered in the way we live the Lordship of Jesus in everyday actions, feelings, and thoughts. As we strive to be like Christ in our everyday lives, following His life as it

---

18. Ibid., 216.

is recorded in Scripture and enfleshed by subsequent generations of disciples, we are living in a way that honors the Lord. In many ways similar to the Eastern notion of honor and shame, we are living for the honor of someone else, rather than the self. Of course, this may seem strange, since it would appear we are honoring Jesus, not the Father. Further, the way in which we accomplish honorable activities is through the power of the Holy Spirit, so aren't we finally bringing honor to Him first? In order to answer this dilemma, allow me to sketch a brief theology of human sanctification and its relationship to the Triune nature of God's activity within Himself and in history.

It is true that we accomplish any acts of righteousness through the Holy Spirit. The human character qualities we identify as Godly are a result of His work in our hearts, minds, and actions. The fruit of the Spirit (Gal 5:22–23) is but a consequence of His activity through direct influence *on* humans and indirect influence *through* humans. In order to understand how this brings honor to the Father we must first see how it brings honor to the Son. The Holy Spirit leads us in the path of living Christlike lives. He grants us the capacity and knowledge to accomplish thinking, feeling, and acting in ways that are like the life of Jesus as it is reflected for us in Scripture. Jesus and the Father sent the Spirit as a Helper (John 14:16, 16:7), but not as a Helper to make our lives easier. His help is directed specifically at producing in us the character of Christ so that we may honor the Son. Jesus Himself clarifies this for us when He, speaking of the Spirit, claims, "He shall glorify Me" (John 16:14). The work of the Spirit in human lives is meant to bring honor to the Son.

The Son's work on the earth was to bring honor to the Father, which He did through His fulfillment of the Father's will. Jesus's life and death were all part of the greater plan to magnify the Father's reputation (John 17:1–5). The Father is now, in turn bringing honor to the Son by establishing His Lordship on the earth. This is not a Lordship that is permeating, at least, not yet. Instead, it is a Lordship expressed in the righteousness of the church displayed before all creation. Indeed, even the angels are an audience to the way in which God is perfecting His reputation in the universe through His work with humans in salvation on the earth (1 Pet 1:12).[19]

---

19. The story of Job in Scripture is best read in this way as well. It starts out with the discussion between God and Satan in heaven. The stage is set for God to display His glory through and to Job. Unfortunately, we are not told the end of the story. Certainly, we know what happened to Job, but we don't get to hear the final conversation between God

The Earth Is My Footstool

By honoring the Son through the Son's posterity, the Father is returning honor to Himself. After all, He is the One who designed the plan "before the foundation of the world" (Eph 1:4). Jesus recognized this, even in the face of His crucifixion.

> Now My soul has become troubled; and what shall I say, "Father save Me from this hour?" But for this purpose I came to this hour. Father, glorify Your name. There came therefore a voice out of heaven: I have both glorified it, and will glorify it again." (John 12:27-28)

This community of persons, Father, Son, and Holy Spirit, takes priority over the individual person, even to the point of making the individual expendable for the sake of the community. Jesus laid down His life for the sake of God's honor. The honor of the Triune community came first, especially the honor of the Father, before Jesus's right to self and the glory that was and is due the Son. With this example of the Triune Godhead in mind, let us look a bit further into how honor functions in relation to God's overall redemptive plan. It is important to notice that though we are not primary in the story, we do play a vital role. God has entrusted us with His reputation, and He will see to it that His honor is clearly seen by all.

Jesus's Lordship is a Lordship established on His honor. In other words, the foundation on which His Lordship is built is the honor of His name found in the righteousness of His body, the church. Certainly His Incarnation, holy life, and sacrificial death exalted Him as the One who is able to be seated at God's right hand—a position of honor. What is being established now is His universal Lordship. In reality, His Lordship is not in question, since God is moving history to accomplish the establishment of His universal kingship (Heb 1:3-13). However, it is not yet displayed in every corner of the universe. Thus, we see the purpose of the church. The human activity of the church is to bring honor to the reputation of the Father by living Christlike lives before a watching world (Phil 2:13). This is not the same thing as establishing a kingdom on earth where Christians control society. Instead, it is life in a community that witnesses the coming universal Lordship of Jesus by living it in everyday ways and testifying of His return to establish it forever. Make no mistake; THE KINGDOM

---

and Satan. Perhaps no conversation occurred. Indeed, who could possibly answer back to God after He speaks His glory to Job in Job 38-41. My point is simply that perhaps the primary audience for the story of Job is not people, but angelic beings, both good and evil.

BELONGS TO JESUS and HE WILL ESTABLISH IT. Jesus will finally establish His Lordship in the end of time. Eschatological literature affirms this for us throughout. His Lordship is sure, but it is not fully expressed or confirmed until the end.[20] Jesus exclaims in Matt 28:18, "All authority has been given to Me in heaven and on earth." He has all authority over all the universe. At the same time, He is patiently awaiting the establishment of His throne in the confines of history, which will finally be accomplished in the eschaton.

Human participation in this process is both reflective and comprehensive. It is reflective in that by living like Christ, Christians reflect honor onto Him, and subsequently, onto the Triune Godhead. It is comprehensive in that Christians also are given honor as they are raised to a life of Godly inheritance. Paul concludes in Rom 8:16–17:

> The Spirit Himself bears witness with our spirit that we are children of God, and if children, heirs also, heirs of God and fellow heirs with Christ, if indeed we suffer with Him in order that we may also be glorified with Him.

Our honor is a shared or derived honor, but it is honor nonetheless. This is the doctrine of glorification. Of course, Piper is right in pointing out that our incentive for pursuing Godliness is not to receive this honor, but because of the great joy discovered in God Himself.[21]

The difficulty in Piper's conception of attributing glory to God is that he strives to maintain the primacy of the individual in the process. Certainly he recognizes that it is insufficient to pursue joy in God and seek to affirm His supremacy without interacting with others. In fact he explicitly takes issue with what he calls the "cult of self."[22] However, the difference to which I am pointing is more foundational than how one cares about others, though this is by no means unimportant. I wish to argue that God has chosen to honor Himself first and foremost through

---

20. Wolfhart Pannenberg develops more fully what may be called a "proleptic" understanding of the establishment of the Triune Lordship over all history and creation. Only at the consummation of history will the reality of God's universal Lordship be confirmed. God's Lordship is never in doubt throughout history, but at the same time, it is somewhat obscured by history. The eschaton will finally grant all creation the fullness of His Lordship. See Wolfhart Pannenberg, *Systematic Theology*, vol. 1, trans. by Geoffrey W. Bromiley (Grand Rapids: Eerdmans, 1991) esp. 327–36.

21. Piper, *Desiring God*, 215–16.

22. Ibid., 251–57.

His church, which takes precedence over the self. In ways similar to how Christ gave Himself for the sake of the Triune God's honor, so too individual believers must give their lives for the sake of Christ's body. Piper's hedonism remains centered on personal joy/happiness and individual holiness. In other words, the church seems to be missing in Piper's model. Why is this a problem?

As alluded to already, individual autonomy creates an environment in which the individual is convinced of his/her capacity for self-determination. Various "rights" and points of control are inherent in such a notion. The problem arises when we begin to ask how God and His supreme sovereignty fit into such an understanding of the self. In a Western democratic environment, steeped as it is in Enlightenment philosophy, the self always takes precedence. God may have influence or give some input to the Western individual, but He is not in control. In the name of preserving human freedom, we have tamed God, bringing Him down to the level of humanity to be dealt with as our equal. Scripture directs our attention elsewhere: to the supreme power and control of God (e.g., Job 38–40; Prov 21:1); as well as to the importance of others above the self (Phil 2:4). The church is critical to God's honor because He has entrusted His reputation to how the church lives His Lordship in its life *as church*.

Scripture seems to focus much of its attention on the community of believers who are called to function as a unit—a body (e.g., 1 Cor 12:12–31). Such a conception of communal identity furthers the notion of honor defined primarily in a group context (i.e., the honor—shame model). We have already seen that the community of the Triune God forms the object of honor. The body of believers known as church forms the substance used to accomplish this honor. The individual becomes defined primarily by participation in the church. Christians become, quite literally, "members one of another" (Rom 12:5). The accountability and formation encountered in living as a community of honor are precisely the marks of how individuals are transformed into parts of the whole. In other words, the individual is subsumed in the larger whole of the community. The process by which God has chosen to form humans into the image of Christ, and thus draw honor to His reputation is what's known in biblical terms as discipleship. It is the patterning of one life onto another, ultimately patterning after the life of Jesus; however, it is not an affirmation of individual holiness above the holiness of the body. Instead, it is an organic process by which the whole is made holy and regarded as one unit—as a body or bride (1 Cor 12; Rom 12:4–5; Rev 19:7–8). The whole is far greater than the sum total of its parts.

The apostle Paul conceived of his role as a master who was apprenticed by the best (Jesus) and who was in turn apprenticing other believers in the Christlikeness meant to point to the holy character of God. "Imitate me as I imitate Christ" (1 Cor 11:1) was his invitation for believers to pattern their lives after the human examples of holiness found in history. It is a call still alive today as more mature believers invite those new to the faith to grow and mature into "vessels of honor" (Rom 9:21; 2 Tim 2:20–21), to become contributing parts of the body. The church is God's instrument for accomplishing the honor He wishes His people to experience and display. In many ways similar to the cultures of honor and shame, the church functions to assist believers in understanding the implications of their lives and actions on God's reputation and the greater body of believers as they become a community of honor. Further, just as the Eastern community experiences honor and shame due to the activities of the individual, so too the church is held accountable for the activities of one person in their midst (1 Cor 5–6, especially 6:5 where Paul calls attention to their shame because the Corinthians have no one in the church capable of judging a civil matter, let alone the spiritual matter just described in chapter 5). Likewise their honor and shame may be bound together and treated as though it was that of an individual (Rev 2–3).

As an aside, it is unfortunate the way the church has lost her vision for character formation according to the model of apprenticeship in Scripture called discipleship. In our modern ethic of making choices according to principles, the New Testament record of Jesus's life has been reduced to the level of another law like the Law of Moses. His actions and attitudes are consequently translated into a list of rules, rather than enfleshed in the lives of believers who model His character. In such a context, discipleship becomes more of an equation where character is the matching of principles to circumstance, making choices by weighing consequences. I fear westerners will never be able to recover a conception of honor as long as we remain committed to the individualistic ethic of choice, underwritten by our presumption of autonomy. We are comfortable with applying rules, rather than attempting to change the heart and character in ways that will conform our whole being. The rules are simply a lot easier and more straightforward. I am quite convinced that in our current evangelical ethos, we would have stoned the woman caught in adultery (John 8:1–11). As a point of fact, we generally still do. The only difference is that as modern assassins, we use our tongues instead of rocks, and we do it in private.

God is honored when His people display an honorable character. When they sin, He disciplines them so that they might be made to "share His holiness" (Heb 12:10). His objective is to create a community that is a pure and holy testimony to His reputation (Ezek 36:22–27). This testimony brings honor to God, and is honoring to the church as well as she fulfills her role in God's plan. In contrast to the typical American understanding of the self, the community of church takes precedence over the individual. Therefore, honor is taught and sought after as a testimony or witness to what is taking place in the church, which is, of course, a testimony to what God is doing in the church (cf. Matt 18:15–20). To bring honor to the life of the church is to bring honor to God, since He created the church and still operates within her as her lifeblood. The communal honor that the church has to offer back to God is the objective of her existence, her *raison d'etre*. Paul seems to regard this as the primary goal of what Christ is doing in the church.

> Husbands, love your wives, just as Christ also loved the church and gave Himself up for her, so that He might sanctify her, having cleansed her by the washing of water with the word, that He might present to Himself the church in all her glory, having no spot or wrinkle or any such thing; but that she would be holy and blameless. (Eph 5:25–27)

It is in the context of corporate life that believers need to dedicate themselves to producing character worthy of God's honor. As moderns, we have finally treated Paul's metaphor of the church as Jesus's "body" too metaphorically. It is more literal than we have been willing to embrace.

THE HAPPINESS OF GRACE

The question that remains is "What does it matter if the church honors God?" Scripture clearly teaches that the church is designed to do such a task. The moral guidance given to the church in the Bible is directed to this end. However, it is just as apparent that God does not *need* anything from His creation in order to be complete in His being and satisfied in His own love for Himself within the Triune relationship. God is self-sufficient; He has within Himself all that He needs to be God. Isaiah 40:12–17 proclaims the fact that God needed no one to teach Him or give Him counsel in His ways. Speaking through Asaph, the Lord declares in Ps 50:10–12, "For every beast of the forest is Mine, the cattle on a thousand hills. I know every bird of the mountains, and everything that moves in the field is Mine. If I were hungry, I would not tell you; for the world is Mine, and all it contains." The authors of the New Testament did not overlook this notion. Preaching to the Greeks at Athens, the apostle Paul confirms that "The God who made the world and all things in it, since He is Lord of heaven and earth, does not dwell in temples made with hands; neither is He served by human hands, as though He needed anything, since He Himself gives to all life and breath and all things..." (Acts 17:24–25). Here Paul is relying on the truth of God's self-sufficiency to demonstrate to the Athenians that their belief in a god who is over all and everything, is an appropriate belief about the God of the Bible.

Further, God is entirely happy in Himself. He delights in the work that He has done and is doing. Piper rightly draws attention to the fact that "God is God—that he is perfect and complete in himself, that he is overflowingly happy in the eternal fellowship of the Trinity, and that he does not need us to complete his fullness and is not deficient without us."[23] This does not mean that God is aloof, or unwilling to share Himself. His great love, His unconditional love, is at the very core of His being. He shares Himself with His creation because He wants us to have the best He has to offer; He is the best that He can give us. God's greatest gift to His creation is Himself. Of course, this same love that is shared with His creation is also the love He shares within Himself as the Triune God. He loves Himself so much that He will not settle for less than what is best for Himself as God. Indeed, by the very definition of His being God, He must be the center of His passion.

> *He* is the center of the gospel. The exaltation of *his* glory is the driving force of the gospel. The gospel is a gospel of *grace*! And grace is the pleasure of God to magnify the worth of God by giving sinners the right and power to delight in God without obscuring the glory of God.[24]

Piper continues throughout his study to demonstrate that human delight in God not only avoids obscuring God's glory; it is the substance

---

23. John Piper, *The Pleasures of God* (Portland: Multnomah, 1991) 18–19.
24. Ibid., 19. Emphasis Piper's.

of His glory in His creation. God has committed Himself to revealing His glory in history through the delight we find in His Lordship. Obedience becomes a natural response to such delight. As Piper notes, "Obedience is the irrepressible public relations project of those who have tasted and seen that the Lord is good (Matt 5:16)."[25]

God's grace is the result of His love. This is love for His creation, but an even greater love compels Him: love for Himself. As explained already, God's honor is paramount in creation history. He loves Himself within the Triune fellowship so deeply that He will not settle for a compromise of each of the Triune person's glory. In other words, the primary objective of the Father's love is to glorify the Son as He molds history into a story of the Son's glory (Heb 1:1–13). The Spirit participates in this glory as the heirs of salvation are brought to glorification (Rom 8:16–17). Finally the Father is glorified as history consummates His universal plan, Son and Spirit fulfilling their mission within creation (economic Trinity) and demonstrating their role as lovers of the Father and one another (ontological Trinity).[26] Therefore, the love of God for His creation is demonstrated as He draws the universe to bow in worship before Him. The love of God for Himself compels Him to draw all history unto His own, rightly deserved, honor.

GOD'S GRACE IN UNIVERSAL RELIEF

The awe-inspiring comprehensiveness of God's honor and grace is discovered as we observe the universal nature of His grace leading to a final universal proclamation of His honor. His grace extends to sinners who are unworthy of His kindness (Rom 5:8). Salvation of sinners is the well-known and widely revered aspect of God's grace. It is often the only aspect of God's grace upheld for praise amongst His people. It is rightly due all the praise we can muster, but let us not forget other objects of His grace. It was noted above that God's grace extends to all creation, including both

---

25. Ibid., 20.

26. For those who may be interested in the doctrine of the Trinity, I am here relying on "Rahner's Rule" that the ontological Trinity *is* the economic Trinity (see Karl Rahner, *Theological Investigations*, IV [London, 1966] 94ff.). There is no difference between the Trinity's person and mission. Indeed, God's mission is His person. I am simply expanding it to demonstrate how His person also reflects His greatest concern to bring honor to Himself. The Triune ontology is rooted in love, but it is a love that both sacrifices and promotes the honor of the other persons within the Trinity.

believers and unbelievers, in that "He Himself gives to all life and breath and all things" (Acts 17:25). A question I am often asked when confronted by the fact that God allows good things to occur for both believers and unbelievers is "Why did God choose to reveal His grace in this way?" "Couldn't He have done it in a 'better' way?" My response is that we don't know the half of it. Let's reflect for a moment on the implications of some passages that extol His grace.

In Jesus's accounting of believers and unbelievers in the end times, He indicates that a separation will occur between the sheep and the goats (Matt 25:31–46). During this judgment of who are the true believers and who are not, Jesus makes some interesting statements regarding eternity. Regarding the "goats" He says, "Depart from Me, accursed ones, into the eternal fire which has been prepared for the devil and his angels" (v. 41). Later in the text, He again relates, "these will go away into eternal punishment, but the righteous into eternal life" (v. 46). We see the prophetic reality of Jesus's words played out in their finality in Rev 20:7–15 where "The devil who deceived them was thrown into the lake of fire and brimstone, where the beast and false prophet are also; and they will be tormented day and night forever and ever" (v. 10). Later in the passage, unbelievers are also added to the lake of fire, due to their unbelief as it is expressed in sinful deeds (v. 15). Two significant points stand out concerning this passage.

First, God is the one who "prepared" the lake of fire, and He is the One who carries out the judgment and punishment on its inhabitants. This is an aspect of God's character sometimes disregarded, prone as we are to think of God as only "good." Of course, God is always and only "good," so how could such a notion of judgment and punishment possibly be regarded as good? Indeed, as will be seen in the following paragraphs, I wish to argue that this judgment and punishment is a mark of His grace. God's goodness is here expressed to Himself as He displays the honor of His wrath in judgment. In other words, creation may not be the center of how good is defined. Before leaving the thought of God creating the lake of fire and punishing those within it, we must press the point further of how God's judgment is not the antithesis of His grace. God's grace is still alive in hell in the fact that hell's inhabitants are not annihilated. They will experience and proclaim worship to God, even while they are not willing to make or deserving of such a proclamation. God's punishment and judgment does not leave them outside the realm of His honor and grace, but it does instigate an altogether different relationship with them. Allow me to move to the second point to explain.

Again in regard to the lake of fire, no mention is made of an end or escape from God's judgment and punishment. All of God's enemies are finally defeated and brought into submission and subjection to His authority and Kingship. How could God possibly accomplish this? One answer is to say that God defeats His enemies at the final battle, "Armageddon." It is true that God defeats His enemies at the end of the tribulation period and again at the end of the millennium (Rev 19:11—20:15). However, this defeat is not the only right God has to reign over His enemies. Scripture presents us with a truth even more powerful than God's defeat of His enemies in battle. This truth is found in, among other places, Paul's letter to the Colossians. In Col 1:19-20, the apostle Paul makes a universal claim regarding the atoning sacrifice made by Jesus on the cross.

> For it was the Father's good pleasure for all the fullness to dwell in Him (the Son), and through Him to reconcile all things to Himself, having made peace through the blood of His cross; through Him, I say, whether things on earth or things in heaven.

Jesus has made peace with "all things" through His atoning work on the cross. These "all things" are the same "all things" created by Him earlier in the passage: "For by Him all things were created, both in the heavens and on earth, visible and invisible, whether thrones or dominions or rulers or authorities—all things have been created by Him and for Him" (1:16). Jesus's sacrificial shedding of His blood on the cross reconciled all things to the Father. This passage does not reflect the manner in which the various things will experience God's reconciliation; it simply states that they are reconciled. Scripture makes it abundantly clear that believers will experience this reconciliation in overwhelmingly joyful ways in eternity as we gather for praise and worship and work in the Father's presence. And as we have seen above, the enemies of God will experience eternal punishment. But the experience of reconciliation is a minor point. The major point here is plainly this: God has claim and sovereign reign over both His children and His enemies due to the atoning work of Christ on the cross. He has every right to judge, since Jesus atoned for all sin and each individual sin as well. Please note the profound implications of this passage. God has reconciled His enemies to Himself through Jesus, which is a stronger right to authority than defeat in battle. Let me put this even more plainly. God has reconciled Satan himself to Himself through Jesus. The Father has made peace with Satan through Jesus, who both created and reconciled Satan to the Father. Remember, "all things have been created by Him and for Him." Even Satan was created for the glory of the Son. Of course, this does not mean that Satan will suddenly "change his stripes" and embrace worship of God as more appropriate than striving against God. *But he will worship God nonetheless.* Paul wrote to the Philippians that because of the Son's humiliation of Himself, the Father is exalting Him above all.

> Therefore also God highly exalted Him, and bestowed on Him the name which is above every name, that at the name of Jesus *every knee should bow*, of those who are in heaven, and on earth, and under the earth, and that *every tongue should confess that Jesus Christ is Lord*, to the glory of God the Father. (Phil 2:9–11, emphasis mine)

Satan and his minions will worship the Son *for eternity* due to the work of the Father through the Son. All God's enemies will be utterly defeated due not only to battle, but even more due to the fact that God has undermined all claims to independence. They will be made a "footstool for [Jesus's] feet" (Heb 2:13). God has rightful claim on all created reality to conform it unto His honor and glory. This He does with believers as they come to embrace His Lordship. He also does this with His enemies as they come to embrace His Lordship in a very different way—judgment and punishment. God will show Himself to be the ultimate King over the entire universe as history reveals His unfailing intentions and plan.

God's grace is expressed in His love for believers and His patience with His enemies. He does not destroy them. He uses them for the sake of demonstrating His glory before all creation. Though this most assuredly seems "unfair" to our political sensibilities, it is nonetheless God's grace to preserve all His creation for the sake of His honor. Nothing and no one goes to waste in the economy of His worship. Fairness is a doctrine based in human presumption, not in biblical anthropology. God treats humans according to His grace and with the purpose of displaying His own Kingship. We may embrace this or rebel, but God will magnify His reputation either way. The focus for believers in understanding His grace is God's kindness. The focus for His enemies is God's patience. In both scenarios, God's grace is evident. Likewise, in both scenarios His grace results in the magnification of His reputation. The goal of God's gracious work in the universe is finally His own honor.[27]

Now we can see the purpose and power of God's politics. He moves to draw all creation unto His glory, but He exerts His authority in a kindness unseen in human politics. He causes believers within the church to act as His ambassadors as they live and move in the world. Indeed, He entrusts His reputation to their existence, though He is constantly working in their midst to bring His own honor about. No doubt can be raised concerning the universal affirmation of His Lordship; it is sure. The power of His politics is the power of love and service. The Son Himself exhibited the sacrifice of service by becoming human and pursuing the reputable life of honor to the Father. Jesus's disciples follow in His footsteps as they sacrifice their lives to His glory in the church. Individuality is offered on the altar of God's honor, where the reputation of God in His church is more important than personal desires or "rights." This is the politics that will finally culminate in the universal embrace of His Kingdom. As will be seen in the next chapter, the honor of this Kingdom is worth giving everything, even our very lives, or perhaps better, especially our lives.

In one of Shakespeare's lesser-known plays, *All's Well that Ends Well*, the playwright weaves a story of a woman who is offered by the king the selection of any eligible bachelor in the king's kingdom. She chooses the man for whom she has had an enduring affection, and the king grants her selection. Unfortunately, the man is loath to marry her, since she is beneath his station. He runs away to war, where he chances to meet a fair maiden in a small village. He woos the maiden, who in turn is in collusion with his wife. The man has sworn to his wife that he will not act as her husband unless she somehow obtains his ring and becomes pregnant by him, both of which are impossible to his mind. In a fairly typical Shakespearian fashion, the roles of the maiden and the wife are switched

---

27. It is from the context of His honor that we should approach passages such as Romans 9 as well. It is often understood as unfair, and thus evil, of God to create "vessels of wrath prepared for destruction" (Rom 9:22). However, the focus of the passage is both God's patience and His right to pursue His own honor. Fairness is an expectation we bring to the text. To regard God as evil for creating some for the purpose of judgment misses the point that He is acting according to His purposes of magnifying His own reputation. In light of His position as owner of creation, we should see our rights as expendable. Those who believe God will honor human rights and individual autonomy have not paid enough attention to the Old Testament. E.g., God wouldn't even let Jonah commit suicide.

and the wife obtains the ring and becomes pregnant by her husband, who thinks he is with the maiden. The wife is the hero of the story in the end, since she is the only one who acted honorably. Shakespeare presents her as the hero, because she is the only one who fulfills her God-given role to the satisfaction of morality. The fact that she posed as someone else was not to her detriment, since she did so in order to fulfill what was right. She was honorable in her actions, and she restored honor to all those associated with her as they were finally vindicated or converted by the praiseworthiness of her actions.

What is fascinating about this story is the way in which the concern for honor is finally justified. Indeed, honor is the central theme of the story. Critics often have a hard time identifying the significance or point of this work of Shakespeare. I suspect this is due to two reasons. First, I would not expect critics to be aware of the allusions to the biblical vernacular prevalent in Shakespeare's day. Though no reference is made by Shakespeare to the similarity, *All's Well that Ends Well* seems to be a wonderful depiction of the story of Judah and Tamar in Scripture (Gen 38). The biblical account of Tamar also depicts her as a hero in that she was more inclined than Judah to fulfill God's Law. When the entire plot is discovered, Judah exclaims, "She is more righteous than I" (38:26). In fact, so great is her honor that she is listed in the genealogy of Jesus in the Gospel of Matthew (1:3). Far from being chastised for her pretense, instead she is hailed as honorable before the Lord for her willingness to go to great lengths to accomplish God's will.

The most interesting connection between these two stories is not the parallelism of the events. The moral of the story seems to be more in view in Shakespeare's intentions, which should perhaps also be the focus when reading the biblical story as well. The second reason critics of Shakespeare's plays have difficulty with *All's Well that Ends well* is due to this ancient and foreign concept of honor. The honorable character of the woman in each story may surprise us when viewed from our Western perspective. We are uneasy about attributing honor to a woman who poses as a prostitute. However, that seems to be exactly what Scripture proposes. Tamar was honorable in doing what she had to do to fulfill the Lord's clear instructions in the Law. Judah recognized this. Perhaps Shakespeare's critics miss it, even as we often miss the nature of honor in Scripture as well.

CONCLUSION

Westerners have difficulty understanding the notion of honor in our contemporary context. The legal worldview of what is right or wrong seems to permeate much of Western life. The individualism of the West makes it likewise difficult to relate to the notion of how a person's actions and life can reflect on the larger group. In this chapter, we saw how Muller's understanding of Eastern cultures helps us re-think how our actions might be interpreted as reflecting on another. As parents, we may be able to relate to this with regard to our children. When they do foolish things, we are embarrassed (shame). When they do honorable things, we are proud of them and feel as though they are reflecting learned values. However, even more important than our relationship with children and parents, or tribe, is our relationship to the Lord of the universe. Piper helped us understand the ultimate importance of always seeing our lives through the paradigm of God's glory. Our goal as humans should be to pursue God with our whole being so that we may discover our greatest delight. Our highest joy is to know Him and be known by Him. In pursuing Him and delighting in Him we fulfill our created purpose of bringing honor to Him as the supreme being in the universe. All history will culminate in the final proclamation of His Lordship. Though the world currently does not reflect His supremacy, He will finally be seen in the end of time as the only One worthy of the Lordship He now has and will have for eternity. God's grace, expressed in His love and patience, grounds the history of the universe as He carefully completes His plan for the ages. All of creation will come to recognize and embrace His rightful authority as the whole universe expresses its worship for all of eternity. The church now lives the reality of the Kingship of Jesus that *all* will know one day. God's politics are of a different order altogether!

SIX

The Performance of a Lifetime

The Politics of Dying Well

God's greatness will triumph both historically and over each person. This is a comforting thought to those who suffer and crawl through the pains of a life marked by torture or torment. Christians around the world testify by their scars that life as a believer is not always pleasant. The apostle Paul promised believers they would be rewarded for their faith with crowns and a great sense of satisfaction at living and dying for the sake of the honor due the Lord (2 Tim 4:7–8). At the same time, he also promised them they would experience persecution in this life, "And indeed, all who desire to live Godly in Christ Jesus will be persecuted" (2 Tim 3:12). God's greatness and His glory still triumph over persecution and martyrdom; but to put it plainly, it is not nearly so pleasant as a life of ease.

When I occasionally find myself speaking on the subject of martyrdom, it is difficult to attain a sense of empathy from American Christians. We cannot resonate with those who are tortured for their faith, and perhaps are even killed for following after Jesus. It is not a surprise that we find it difficult to relate. We have hardly experienced any persecution in America for our faith. Further, death seems a ludicrous option when we have such peace and safety in a free country to worship and believe as we wish.

I do not blame people for being attracted to peace and safety. Paul tells us to pray for it (1 Tim 2:1–2). Indeed, I do not wish for my own children to experience persecution or death for their faith. However, I fear the possibility of losing the willingness, even the desire, to honor Christ with my death, albeit an untimely one. It seems American evangelicals have lost the boldness of the early church (and churches elsewhere today) as we have become more comfortable in living here in this world. The question that seems most perplexing for American Christians is not why we find it difficult to embrace suffering and martyrdom, though that is a question worth pursuing further below. The more pressing question for us is, "Why do we *not* experience persecution in America?"

The answer to this question is at once ideological and practical. The ideological assumption is that the lack of persecution, at least physically harmful persecution, is due to the maintenance of the ideal of religious liberty. This is certainly partly true. Religious liberty and the court system have kept generations from being tortured. We do not suffer persecution because the established laws of the land have not allowed it. At the same time, freedom of religion has caused believers to embrace the notion that being protected from persecution is not merely the preferable option; it is the only option, which is a type of coercion by the state. The state has convinced us that freedom of religion is a necessity for the church to carry out its mission well.

Of course, believers know that religious freedoms are fleeting and can be lost as quickly as they were gained. For the sake of practicality in the West, the state has been slow in challenging and, at times, even revoking religious liberties, because the benefit to the state is minimal. Currently, the state has the church in a position that is extremely advantageous to itself. The church has become convinced by the state that life in this world, at least a life that fulfills certain assumptions about happiness, is preferable to life in the next. Thus, the commitment of the church to securing the success of the state remains quite high. In regard to the state, the church sees its role as producing contributing citizens, so that the church's comfortable relationship with the state might continue; the church has become an arm of the state. This is true to such an extent that the church's "propping up" of the state rivals her goal to produce worshipers who are willing to die for their faith commitment. In other words, the church is currently not dangerous enough for the state to persecute. To put it in biblical language, Jesus promised the world would hate believers precisely because we are not of the world. "If the world hates you, you know that it has hated Me before it hated you. If you were of the world, the world would love its own; but because you are not of the world, but I chose you out of the world, therefore the world hates you" (John 15:18–19). America does not hate the church because we are best regarded by it as an ally, rather than a rival. In other words, America has tamed the church, and in the process has caged the power of witness she once had. This domestication of the church has occurred as people have become satisfied with life in this world and no longer long for the next life with the same passion as those whose lives are in peril; those who regard themselves as hated. Now, the American church's goal seems to be to ride the wave of safe Christianity as long as we possibly can.

By no means do I wish to imply that persecution of the church is absent from this generation in America. Instead, the persecution is more subtle and occurs as the church commits itself to ideologies and practicalities that make life for the church safer and easier. Persecution of the American church comes in the form of distractions and commitments that seem harmless, or at least complementary to the purposes of the church. As John MacArthur points out, "When the church is politicized, even in support of good causes, its spiritual power is vitiated and its moral influence diluted."[1] As we have already observed, the church's commitment to freedom has drawn her into campaigning and fund-raising for the sake of establishing a semblance of the kingdom here on earth prior to the return of Christ. In other words, the American evangelical church seems to have concluded that life in this world is an end in itself, rather than a means to an end. What a contrast to the world of the church for the first few centuries of her existence and to the church in many parts of the world today.

CHILDREN IN HARM'S WAY

Parents should never outlive their children. Those who have lost children know the painful reality of dreaming about their future, even years after they are gone from this earth. Our desire to protect and provide for our children is God's gift to us as we deeply love them and give ourselves to them, beckoning them to maturity in Christ. We think it a difficulty to ask of anyone that they should give their lives for a cause, but to put a child in harm's way seems sadistic to us here in America today. Our fear is borne out of our belief that life is precious and is to be preserved at all costs, especially when such lives have not yet reached their full potential. However, it seems Scripture sees the value of life from a different paradigm.

Jeremiah is warned in Jer 16:1–2, "The word of the Lord came to me saying, 'You shall not take a wife for yourself nor have sons or daughters

---

1. MacArthur, *Romans 9–16*, 207.

in this place.'" God gave him this warning because God was pronouncing judgment on His people who denied and rejected Him. The sons and daughters born in Judah would die early deaths due to disease, along with their mothers and fathers (16:3-4). The world is occasionally a dangerous place into which to bring children. God's judgment was clear to Jeremiah, making it plain why children didn't belong in the world of his day. Unfortunately, we have no such knowledge of the future today. We cannot see what awaits the next generation. Our impulse is to protect them by providing a better world in which to live—a safer world. Parents lie awake at night, worrying over the possibility we may not be able to provide these things.

The optimism about the world of the next generation may or may not be warranted based on history. When the Lord warned Jeremiah of impending judgment, his only hope, and that of the people, was to repent and turn to God in faith and obedience. Jesus warned His disciples "And do not fear those who kill the body, but are unable to kill the soul; but rather fear Him who is able to destroy both soul and body in hell" (Matt 10:28). Both the Old Testament and the New Testament affirm that fear of the Lord, that is, a reverent submission to His supremacy, is more important than life, whether young or old. No inevitability of progress becomes apparent in our reading of biblical history; in fact, the opposite seems the case. The world is not naturally becoming safer. Unfortunately, with regard to children, we are sometimes shortsighted by thinking God's sovereignty is a doctrine for mature people whose life course is already clarified. Though it is certainly true that children do not yet know their careers or mates, God's supremacy is to be embraced by all generations. The importance of honoring the Lord in our lives and our deaths always outweighs our own desires or pursuits, even our own existence. We need to see the world as a dangerous place for all who wish to live a life of honor to the Lord, even for children.

Children are often valued, especially in America, for their potential. In other words, children are valuable precisely for their future abilities or place in society. Mothers and fathers long for their maturity so we can relate to them as peers. The culture looks for and rewards their contribution to the social fabric of their school, neighborhood or city. The government values them based on their eventual contribution to the Gross National Product (GNP). When children die, everyone feels slighted due to some potential that has been lost. However, Scripture does not value life based on future potential. Scripture looks at the past and present and determines value based on God's economy. The prophet Jeremiah knew of God's intimate knowledge of his life. God spoke to him at the beginning of his ministry: "Before I formed you in the womb, I knew you, and before you were born I consecrated you; I have appointed you a prophet to the nations" (Jer 1:5). These words of God's intimate knowledge of His creation were affirmed generations earlier by David the king as he pondered his own existence.

> For Thou didst form my inward parts;
> Thou didst weave me together in my mother's womb.
> I will give thanks to Thee, for I am fearfully and wonderfully made;
> Wonderful are Thy works,
> And my soul knows it very well.
> My frame was not hidden from Thee,
> When I was made in secret,
> And skillfully wrought in the depths of the earth.
> Thine eyes have seen my unformed substance;
> And in Thy book they were all written,
> The days that were ordained for me,
> When as yet there was not one of them. (Ps 139:13–16)

Life is valuable in so far as it is understood in these terms: *known by God*. The implication of this, of course is that all life is valuable, since God knows all people and all things. However, what is important for our discussion is that we understand life as valuable because God has made it, not because of the person's contribution to the GNP. The honor of living for God does not necessitate longevity. It is most certainly sad, even devastating and disastrous when children die, but their short lives are not meaningless. Their contribution to God's glory can be perfected in their life *and* their death, just as it can be for adults. God has numbered their days that they might fulfill His purposes. Each day of their life is a gift *from* Him and a gift *to* Him as it is lived. Their lives must be understood as lived for Him in the same manner as, or at least in a similar manner to, the lives of adults. He is pleased with their fulfillment of His plans and purposes, though at their deaths, we often can hardly see past our own tears. We may never know His purpose in their shortened lives, but we can rest assured that He is never surprised by their death, nor is He disappointed with their existence. This is why it is so critical that we understand His glory and purposes to be the center of all our lives. Any death, including the death of a child, even the death of an infant, only makes sense in the light of His supremacy over all life and all history. Thus, even the most unnecessary of deaths, the martyrdom of children, has the glory of God as a backdrop and the welcoming arms of Jesus as a comfort. The suffering and death of children by other means, such as an accident, is no different; suffering and death still only make sense in view of Jesus's hold on something greater than future existence on this earth, though even then, to us, "making sense" of it all may not be possible.[2]

Perhaps the more critical reason martyrdom remains so foreign to the Western world is that we, as rational adults, are taught to die alone. By this, I am simply pointing to something the euthanasia movement has already discovered and exploited. Western individuals tend to live as though we are in control of our own destiny, constantly denying the sovereignty of God. Living in such a way creates a dilemma when the prospect of death arises. We cannot control the onset of disease or the decay of this mortal flesh. Therefore, we do the closest thing we can to maintain autonomy over death: we embrace it prematurely. All of this is done in the name of personal freedom and dignified control over one's life. Despite the rhetoric, such a death is a death for the sake of self. In other words, though we may think we're doing it because we don't wish to burden others, premature death does not remove the burden. Those who remain are left with the problem of coping with their own exclusion from the process. Whether they were not capable of supporting a friend who suffered greatly, or they were unwilling to embrace suffering and pain in

2. As I write this, the news media are still reporting the amazing story of Charles Roberts IV, who opened fire in a small Amish school in Nickel Mines, PA. After secluding himself with young girls in the school, Roberts shot ten of the children, killing five, and then killed himself. What is incredible about this story is not that a man would perpetrate such evil; sin is ugly in all of its manifestations. What has struck the secular media dumb in the face of this tragedy is the response of the Amish community to the deaths of their children. Only hours after the shooting, people from the community were sadly, but boldly, holding out forgiveness as their response. Further, they contacted Roberts's wife and family to comfort them and offer their sympathy, walking together with the family through the pain and guilt. The world found such a response outrageous, though admirable. Such a reliance on the sovereignty of God was a statement no book or sermon, no explanation, could equal. Christians across the nation were stunned as well. We were stunned because we could not imagine such a faith; stunned because we have been taught by the world a different way to pursue justice; stunned because we have forgotten the very death of Jesus was a silent testimony to God's grace. But here, for perhaps only a few weeks, the world has an opportunity to see the power of the Gospel through a faithful response to martyrdom. This is the rationality of witness.

another, those who remain are left to wonder why someone would die to preserve the wealth and autonomy of the living. Euthanasia, whether active or passive, is but a monument to the selfishness of the living. It appears noble at first glance that one would kill himself for the sake of preventing a burden to others. The great deception is that the hard truth boils down to mere "inconvenience." The dying may be willing to embrace suffering and pain, if they knew they would not have to do it alone.

The greatest answer the church has to such a deception is the reality of her presence. Believers live as the body of Christ. This is more than simply a nice metaphor. We should be a living, moving, functioning organism. Instead, we live separated lives, divided by concerns the world has coerced us into considering ultimate. I won't delve into a developed understanding of the church here; that would take several more chapters. However, one simple point should suffice: The church's greatest ministry is her life as Christ's body. Loving another is always a violation of his/her autonomy; it is always inconvenient. From such a perspective, biblical love is one of the more violent acts we can do, since it is an infringement on the parameters of autonomy well beyond the accepted norms of observing someone's personal rights. Love is seeking the best for another, even when it costs us much and creates opportunities for resentment due to the obvious disregard of privacy. We are called to "re-incarnate" the life of Christ, His self-sacrificing love, in our everyday actions, thoughts, and intentions. Obviously, I am not speaking here of discovering the past lives of reincarnation. Such a notion is biblically ludicrous. What I am saying is that the way we live for the sake of the other is precisely how the church exists as a witness to the world. Jesus's human life was lived, and He died, for the sake of others: "For even the Son of Man did not come to be served, but to serve, and to give His life a ransom for many" (Mark 10:45). Martyrdom is the highest expression of living and dying for the sake of another, for in it we are demonstrating that our lives exist for the sake of witness to Him. This is, or at least should be, the politics of the church. By this, I mean to say that in living as church, we are teaching others that the Lordship of Jesus is higher than the autonomy of the self. Martyrdom teaches us that life and death are Christocentric, that is, "Christ-centered." The lives He has given us and the deaths He brings to us are but a means of expressing His Supremacy over all creation. We die for the sake of another (Jesus), even as we have lived in our existence as church for the sake of another. This is what it means to die well: to die in such a way as to draw attention to the reputation of Jesus. Though a very foreign concept to Western individualism, such a notion is not at all foreign to the church.

LIFE IN THE FACE OF DEATH

Justin the Martyr, one of the early church Fathers, did not shrink back from confessing his Lord when faced with possible persecution and death. Rusticus the Roman prefect presiding over Justin's trial, asked him plainly, "Are you not, then, a Christian?" Justin's simple response, "Yes, I am a Christian." resulted in a sentence of death.[3] He did not shrink back, nor did he plead for leniency. He went to his death knowing something better awaited him. At Justin's trial, other believers were also present who died with him. Their responses to the questions of Rusticus reveal a rather compelling perspective on death by the early church.

> Rusticus the prefect said, "Where do you assemble? "Justin said, "Where each one chooses and can: for do you fancy that we all meet in the very same place? Not so; because the God of the Christians is not circumscribed by place; but being invisible, fills heaven and earth, and everywhere is worshipped and glorified by the faithful." Rusticus the prefect said, "Tell me where you assemble, or into what place do you collect your followers? "Justin said, "I live above one Martinus, at the Timiotinian Bath; and during the whole time (and I am now living in Rome for the second time) I am unaware of any other meeting than his. And if any one wished to come to me, I communicated to him the doctrines of truth." Rusticus said, "Are you not, then, a Christian? "Justin said, "Yes, I am a Christian."
>
> Then said the prefect Rusticus to Chariton, "Tell me further, Chariton, are you also a Christian? "Chariton said, "I am a Christian by the command of God." Rusticus the prefect asked the woman Charito, "What say you, Charito? "Charito said, "I am a Christian by the grace of God." Rusticus said to Euelpistus, "And what are you? "Euelpistus, a servant of Caesar, answered, "I too am a Christian, having been freed by Christ; and by the grace of Christ I partake of the same hope." Rusticus the prefect said to Hierax, "And you, are you a Christian? "Hierax said, "Yes, I am a Christian, for I revere and worship the same God." Rusticus the prefect said, "Did Justin make you Christians? "Hierax said, "I

---

3. The quotations of Rusticus and Justin are taken from Alexander Roberts and James Donaldson, editors, "The Martyrdom of the Holy Martyrs," *The Ante-Nicene Fathers*, vol. 1 (Grand Rapids: Eerdmans, 1996) ch. 2, 305.

was a Christian, and will be a Christian." Paeon stood up and said "I too am a Christian." Rusticus the prefect said, "Who taught you?" Paeon said, "From our parents we received this good confession." Euelpistus said, "I willingly heard the words of Justin. But from my parents I also learned to be a Christian." Rusticus the prefect said, "Where are your parents?" Euelpistus said, "In Cappadocia." Rusticus says to Hierax, "Where are your parents? "And he answered, and said, "Christ is our true father, and faith in Him is our mother; and my earthly parents died; and I, when I was driven from Iconium in Phrygia, came here." Rusticus the prefect said to Liberianus, "And what say you? Are you a Christian, and unwilling to worship [the gods]? "Liberianus said, "I too am a Christian, for I worship and reverence the only true God." . . . Rusticus the prefect pronounced sentence, saying, "Let those who have refused to sacrifice to the gods and to yield to the command of the emperor be scourged, and led away to suffer the punishment of decapitation, according to the laws." The holy martyrs having glorified God, and having gone forth to the accustomed place, were beheaded, and perfected their testimony in the confession of the Saviour.[4]

Several intriguing points stand out about this quote. Obviously, the bravery of these believers is without question. Further, their openness to martyrdom and the martyrdom of others is captivating. Paeon and Euelpistus "sell out" Justin and their parents as the ones who taught them to be Christians and to refuse sacrifice to the Roman gods. They were not being coerced into such a confession, as though remaining alive could convince them to bear witness against those who taught them the faith. Instead, they willingly gave names and places, so that all, even Rusticus, would know the source of their learning. They gave this information even while knowing they would die, whether they gave it or not. One could easily surmise that things did not go well for their parents. The only reason for willingly giving information regarding the source of their learning to be Christians must have been a conviction that their parents would be willing, and perhaps even desirous, to bear witness through martyrdom as well.

A final observation about the words of Paeon and Euelpistus points to something peculiar about their parents. Why would parents train a child to become a Christian and deny the gods of the Romans when the

4. Ibid., chs. 1–2, 3, 305–6.

possibility of eventual martyrdom was quite likely? Indeed, why would parents wish to have children at all in such a hostile environment? One could easily speculate that perhaps martyrdom was not a reality when these people were first born. However, the text gives no indication that the parents would rescind their goal of training their children to be believers, even in the face of death. Likely, given the response to Rusticus, these martyrs believed their parents would concur with their statements. The most likely answer to why parents would have children and raise them in the faith is that they believed life and death to be a means to a greater end. Witness to Christ and His glorious Lordship, even by the lips of their own martyred children, was a testimony to the death and resurrection of Jesus, a death in which all believers are called to share (Rom 6:3–5; Phil 3:10–11). Raising children seems to have had as its primary goal the confession of Christ in life *and* in death. Though it was a dangerous thing to have children in the midst of martyrdom, it was more dangerous to raise them as though their confession of Christ was optional when faced with peril. Their lives, whether young or old, were expendable for the sake of testimony.

What a fantastic notion—to prepare our children for a shortened future for the sake of witness. This goes against so much of what our culture tells upcoming generations. Even further, it goes against what our parental "instinct" causes us to believe. It appears to us as simply "not right" to forego the possibility of future survival for the sake of something as seemingly trivial as a belief. Of course, the problem with such "instincts" is that they are focused on the only thing humans seem to find valuable: human welfare. Rising above such instincts is exactly what Jesus sought for His followers when He implored them to "take up [their] cross daily" (Luke 9:23; cf. Matt 16:24; Mark 8:34). The repulsiveness of such a statement is lost on our contemporary culture. The cross has become a piece of jewelry worn by many who may or may not associate themselves with Jesus and His teachings. The significance of the cross is largely meaningless in our world today. In Jesus's day, "taking up your cross daily" meant being prepared for and even looking forward to a horrid death on a daily basis. Jesus was asking more than for His followers to sacrifice an occasional desire for His sake, or to bear with some hardship for a time. He was asking them to die. While it may be needed and beneficial that we make sacrifices and bear burdens short of death, Jesus's words should not be dismissed so easily, as though He was *merely* speaking metaphorically.

His own cross bears witness to the fact His words were far more literal than we care to imagine or admit. Jesus calls us to die! We may be granted more days in our short life on earth, but each day should begin with an ever-present reminder that today He asks us to die.

In some ways, children are probably more prepared for accepting such a plight than adults. When Jesus rebukes His disciples for keeping the children from Him (Mark 10:13–16; Luke 18:15–17), He goes on to state, "the kingdom of God belongs to such as these" (Mark 10:14; Luke 18:16). His statement is hardly a reference to age. Instead, He seems to be indicating that the faith and dependence of children should be a hallmark of all believers. What if we define His Kingdom as a Kingdom only entered by death? What if Jesus's expectation is that even children would die as His followers? We have trivialized the call of the cross by making it simply a message of rational belief in the facts of the Gospel. Jesus seems to have a much higher price in mind, perhaps even for children. By no means should the martyrdom of children be trivialized by regarding it as something that simply attends Christian faith in a harsh country. There is no means by which the martyrdom of children can be made palatable. It is a tragedy by all accounts. However, it is a tragedy overshadowed only by faith. The glory of the kingdom entered by martyrs causes all the cares and regrets of a life shortened on earth to be silenced. The Savior's embrace knows no regrets.

The point of our discussion is simply to demonstrate this: Life in this world is a means to the greater end of bringing honor to the reputation of Jesus, and through Him to the Father. Christians have, rightly, placed a high value on life. Life is a gift from God to be lived in a way that brings pleasure to Him, and in so doing, brings us great pleasure as well. Unfortunately, we seem to have overestimated life's value by making it the supreme gift and purpose for our existence. The Gospel presented by today's church is hardly a truth worth dying for! Human happiness and contentment seem to have overshadowed the glory of God in our generation, even as it has in other generations as well. In our Western democracies, war seems the only context in which life becomes expendable. Perhaps this is precisely because life in a democracy has become the supreme utopia for humanity and individual freedom has become our foundational doctrine. The evangelical emphasis on salvation and conversion for the sake of life *after* death may skew our perspective regarding the purpose of mortal existence. Since such an emphasis could teach us that true life will begin after leaving our mortality behind for immortality, the purpose of life prior to death seems open to interpretation. I'm not sure we could say of God with Job "Though He slay me, *yet* I will hope in Him" (Job 13:15). Amid all the benefits of worshiping without persecution, such reticence to make our mortal existence subservient to the supremacy of the Lord seems the curse of freedom.

We have grown quite adept at rehearsing the privileges of being protected from bodily harm for faith in Jesus. We do not seem to recognize what is lost in other ways because of being free from persecution. For the first several generations of the church, believers were very aware that their faith made them a target for the government. Being a disciple of Jesus was not merely a nice thing to do on Sundays, nor was it a way to make life more moral or pleasant, as though handling finances well or being better parents was the purpose of faith. Facing the constant threat of martyrdom for their faith made early believers live every day knowing it could be their last. For those who met the executioner, belief in Jesus was finally all that mattered. It is one thing to die as though Jesus is all that matters; it is another to live in this way, day after day, when death could come at any moment.

IGNATIUS IN THE LAND OF THE LIVING

Tradition tells us that the apostle John lived a normal life span and died of natural causes, after experiencing boiling oil and exile. The other apostles experienced premature deaths at the hands of Roman authorities. The first century church did not know the peace for which Paul prayed and for which he encouraged Timothy to pray (1 Tim 2:1-2). Instead they knew torment, torture, and death as the normative way of life for Christians. Of course, we cannot possibly demonstrate exactly what was the mind of the apostles when they were condemned to beheading, crucifixion, and the like. However, it may be possible to gain some insight into their understanding of suffering and martyrdom through those who followed in their footsteps.

The apostle John left an indelible imprint on the life of the early church. His writing was quickly accepted as an authoritative source for understanding the revelation of God's Son, Jesus. Further, his writing also depicted future events and the closest thing the church has to an explanation regarding why Jesus has not yet returned. Beyond the incredible influence of these writings, John finally left behind several men who were forever impacted by his commitment to the Lord Jesus. One of the better-known disciples of John is another martyr of the early church: Ignatius.

Ignatius's life was spent as a leader in the church. His position at the end of his life was the bishop of Antioch, a position not highly coveted due to the public nature of being a leader in a movement that went against the grain of Roman religion. Ignatius gratefully acknowledged the Lord's sparing of the church under the Roman emperor Trajan, having endured the hardships and persecutions of Domitian. However, his biography, likely recorded by Ignatius's friends who accompanied him to his death in Rome, is not a story of success due to his survival. Instead, Ignatius felt as though he had missed something by remaining alive.

> Wherefore he rejoiced over the tranquil state of the Church, when the persecution ceased for a little time, but was grieved as to himself, that he had not yet attained to a true love to Christ, nor reached the perfect rank of a disciple. For he inwardly reflected, that the confession which is made by martyrdom, would bring him into a yet more intimate relation to the Lord.[5]

Ignatius was no masochist. He simply had a commitment to his life that was secondary to the purposes and honor of the Lord. His life was a means to the end of witness and he wanted his death to speak clearly of the greatness discovered in face to face relationship with the Lord of the universe. Thus, he was pleased when Trajan singled him out for special treatment.

> Then Trajan pronounced sentence as follows: "We command that Ignatius, who affirms that he carries about within him Him that was crucified, be bound by soldiers, and carried to the great [city] Rome, there to be devoured by the beasts, for the gratification of the people." When the holy martyr heard this sentence, he cried out with joy, "I thank thee, O Lord, that Thou hast vouchsafed to honour me with a perfect love towards Thee, and hast made me to be bound with iron chains, like Thy Apostle Paul." Having spoken thus, he then, with delight, clasped the chains about him; and when he had first prayed for the Church, and commended it with tears to the Lord, he was hurried away by the savage cruelty of the soldiers, like a distinguished ram, the leader of a goodly flock, that he

---

5. Alexander Roberts and James Donaldson, editors, "The Martyrdom of Ignatius," *The Ante-Nicene Fathers*, vol. 1 (Grand Rapids: Eerdmans, 1996) ch. 1, 129.

might be carried to Rome, there to furnish food to the bloodthirsty beasts.[6]

How could Ignatius look forward to death, even rejoice in his being bound for the passage to Rome to be delivered up to the beasts? This is not a new question. Certainly, the believers of the first centuries found it strange as well. In the final measure, martyrdom is a learned truth of Christian worship, not a natural product of belief. The learning must come as longing for life with Jesus and a mourning over the temptations and struggles of this world replace our tendency to be at home in this world. The Roman believers of Ignatius's day struggled with losing him to the beasts, just as we likely would be perplexed by a desire for death today. Ignatius comforts and instructs them in his *Epistle to the Romans*, sent as preparatory remarks for his expected martyrdom in Rome.

> For it is not my desire to act towards you as a man-pleaser, but as pleasing God, even as also ye please Him. For neither shall I ever have such [another] opportunity of attaining to God; nor will ye, if ye shall now be silent, ever be entitled to the honour of a better work. For if ye are silent concerning me, I shall become God's; but if you show your love to my flesh, I shall again have to run my race. Pray, then, do not seek to confer any greater favour upon me than that I be sacrificed to God while the altar is still prepared; that, being gathered together in love, ye may sing praise to the Father, through Christ Jesus, that God has deemed me, the bishop of Syria, worthy to be sent for from the east unto the west. It is good to set from the world unto God, that I may rise again to Him.
>
> Ye have never envied anyone; ye have taught others. Now I desire that those things may be confirmed [by your conduct], which in your instructions ye enjoin [on others]. Only request in my behalf both inward and outward strength, that I may not only speak, but [truly] will; and that I may not merely be called a Christian, but really be found to be one. For if I be truly found [a Christian], I may also be called one, and be then deemed faithful, when I shall no longer appear to the world. Nothing visible is eternal. "For the things which are seen are temporal, but the things which are not seen are eternal" (2 Cor 4:18). For our God, Jesus Christ, is all the more revealed [in His glory]. Christianity is not a thing of silence only, but also of [manifest] greatness.
>
> I write to the churches and impress on them all, that I shall willingly die for God, unless ye hinder me. I beseech of you not to

---

6. Ibid., ch. 2, 130.

show an unseasonable good will towards me. Suffer me to become food for the wild beasts, through whose instrumentality it will be granted me to attain to God . . . Entreat Christ for me, that by the [teeth of the wild beasts] I may be found a sacrifice to God.

May I enjoy the wild beasts that are prepared for me; and I pray they may be found eager to rush upon me, which also I will entice to devour me speedily, and not deal with me as with some, whom, out of fear, they have not touched. But if they be unwilling to assail me, I will compel them to do so. Pardon me [in this]: I know what is for my benefit. Now I begin to be a disciple. And let no one, of things visible or invisible, envy me that I should attain Jesus Christ. Let fire and the cross; let the crowds of wild beasts; let tearings, breakings, and dislocations of bones; let cutting off of members; let shatterings of the whole body; and let all the dreadful torments of the devil come upon me: only let me attain to Jesus Christ.

All the pleasures of the world, and all the kingdoms of this earth, shall profit me nothing. It is better for me to die in behalf of Jesus Christ, than to reign over all the ends of the earth. "For what shall a man be profited, if he gain the whole world, but lose his own soul?" (Matt 16:26). Him I seek, who died for us: Him I desire, who rose again for our sake. This is the gain which is laid up for me.

Pardon me brethren: do not hinder me from living, do not wish to keep me in a state of death; and while I desire to belong to God, do not ye give me over to the world. Suffer me to obtain pure light: when I have gone thither, I shall indeed be a man of God. Permit me to be an imitator of the passion of my God . . .

The prince of this world would fain carry me away, and corrupt my disposition towards God. Let none of you, therefore, who are [in Rome] help him; rather be ye on my side, that is on the side of God. Do not speak of Jesus Christ, and yet set your desires on the world . . . For though I am alive while I write to you, I am eager to die.[7]

Such eagerness is a realization that Jesus's Lordship extends beyond the details and circumstances of this life. His authority affords believers the opportunity to be with Him in the end. Ignatius's longings were so strong to be with Jesus that he encouraged the Roman Christians to let him pass from their midst. So strong was his conviction that a martyr's death would grant him a pure testimony to Christ that he desired the "wild beasts" to

---

7. Alexander Roberts and James Donaldson, eds., "Epistle of Ignatius to the Romans," *The Ante-Nicene Fathers*, vol. 1 (Grand Rapids: Eerdmans, 1996) chs. 2–7, 74–76.

leave little or no remains of his earthly body.[8] Far from a Gnostic notion of the evil nature of all things material, Ignatius instead simply did not wish to trouble his friends with caring for his remains.

What is most interesting for our discussion from the lives of Ignatius and Justin is that they both believed martyrdom granted them a status of discipleship given only to those who were willing to face death as a test of their belief in Jesus. The focus was on their testimony to the Lord Jesus and the great reward at perfecting that testimony in death. Preserving their existence was always secondary to knowing Christ.

DEATH IN AMERICA

Talking about death seems a strange and morbid thing in the West. We have done all we can to conquer death in our civilized cultures. Each year, we spend billions of dollars in research to find ways to stave off the end of life. It seems counterproductive to talk of it as though it is inevitable and should be thought through or even embraced in such a way as to convey a meaning beyond itself. Death is meaningless in a culture fashioned around self-pleasure. As a consequence, death in the West has become a secret. We don't talk of it, and we find it poor form if someone does. The drive for preservation in the worship of self makes death the final enemy in everyone's life. Therefore, we craft our lives so that we don't have to face death until the bitter end. Then, at the end, we pity the soul who has lost everything this life has to offer. We have reversed the biblical model. For those in the West who are used to peace and comfort, life is everything; death is the greatest loss. Martyrdom for belief in Jesus seems unfortunate, though perhaps modestly admirable. We eulogize the great accomplishments of the dead at funerals, because we believe legacy to be found in how someone passed the time while living in this world. We see death as a tragic end, rather than a grand opportunity for greater legacy. No test seems to exist for us to demonstrate the quality of "dying well."

The political power of death in the church today is largely discovered only in our avoidance of it. Death is a personal issue, the politics of which is tied to the politics of the self. That's why martyrdom is so foreign; it makes no sense in the world of the self. There is no power in dying for another when the self is all that really matters. Thus, even the death of

---

8. Alexander Roberts and James Donaldson, eds., "The Third Epistle of the Same St. Ignatius," *The Ante-Nicene Fathers*, vol. 1 (Grand Rapids: Eerdmans, 1996) ch. 4, 103.

Jesus *merely* represents a larger principle of love. His death is marked by principle, since the bloody messiness of a sacrificial atonement seems too garish for our liberal sensibilities.

Of course, for believers, life and death are not, or at least should not be, so politically skewed toward the self. Believers live *and die* the Lordship of Jesus before a world who does not know its King. Only in such a context will martyrdom make sense. Indeed, only in such a context will any death make sense. The power of every death is discovered in its witness to a reality larger than life and death in this world. This is the politics of death in the church.

THE POLITICS OF DEATH FOR PAUL AND THE ROMANS

The inflated power of the individual has become galvanized in Western political ideologies. Americans, especially, have become convinced that the power of the self is maintained and protected by the government. Thus, we believe the government is us. We believe we have a vested interest is seeing the government succeed, since the autonomy of the self is at stake. The church has taken its place alongside the rest of America by rooting the foundation of the church in the freedom of the individual. Each person believes in his/her own self-determined right to individuated religious belief—the freedom of religion, which by implication, has led naturally to the privatization of belief. Each person may believe as he/she wishes, which means anyone can believe anything, as long as it does not infringe on another's right to believe. In such a voluntaristic context, it now seems impossible the church could survive without the freedom to determine her own existence. Such notions are rooted in *a priori* commitments to the self. In other words, the church and her existence are subservient commitments to the self and the ideology of autonomy. Christians have gladly sacrificed testimony to God's sovereign control on the altar of self-preservation, rather than sacrificing self for the sake of God's greatness.

Such was not always the case. As we saw above, the first generations of the church anticipated that an early death would accompany faith in Jesus. Those who understood the fleeting nature of mortal existence even longed for the testimony of a faith so enduring and secure that it could face the executioner. The apostle Paul himself longed to be in the presence of Jesus.

The Performance of a Lifetime

> For to me, to live is Christ, and to die is gain. But if I am to live on in the flesh, this will mean fruitful labor for me; and I do not know which to choose. But I am hard-pressed from both directions, having the desire to depart and be with Christ, for that is very much better; yet to remain on in the flesh is more necessary for your sake. (Phil 1:21–23)

Paul desired to be with Christ, which implied undergoing the transformation from this life to the next. Death did not frighten Paul. His reasons for wishing to remain alive centered on the welfare of the Philippians. But he clearly recognized that life with Jesus was preferable to anything life in this world could offer.

When he turned his attention to life in this world in his letter to the Romans, it is hard to imagine the same author penning merely cordial symbiotic existence to the Roman believers regarding their relationship to the governing authorities. It seems outrageous that Paul could long to be in the presence of Jesus and yet advise the Romans as to how they could live with and even become a part of the governing control of culture and country. However, an intentional infiltration of human government is the more common reading of Rom 13:1–7 today amongst some evangelicals.[9] Those who would wish for Christians to claim ownership over the way in which government supervises the evolution of culture often point to this passage as support for Christian "participation" in government.[10] Of course, "participation" is too weak a word for what is desired. Christians, like anyone else playing the game of worldly power, want authority and control, since "We have as much right as anyone else to contend for our views as does any other citizen."[11] Christians typically argue that such authority could, and would, be exercised for the benefit of individuals and society as a whole. In their plea for engaging the political culture, the group commissioned by the National Association of Evangelicals to develop scholarly articles on the subject offered this purpose statement for engagement in the Preamble of their "For the Health of the Nation: An Evangelical Call to Civic Responsibility": "Never before has God given American evangelicals such an awesome opportunity to shape public policy in ways that could contribute to the well-being of the entire world.

---

9. Tom Minnery, *Why You Can't Stay Silent: A Biblical Mandate to Shape Our Culture* (Wheaton, IL: Tyndale, 2001) 55ff.

10. Ibid., 99–100.

11. Ibid., 55.

Disengagement is not an option."[12] Participation easily translates into self-preservation and the common good of all humanity. Such a position is tantamount to having one foot in the church and one foot in the world (ala the Social Gospel). Though it is presented as a complementary position for life as a church devoted to the Lordship of Jesus lived out in a world that is hostile to Him, it turns out to be simply a means to masquerade the competition that really exists between the church and the world. We are finally left with the questions, "Who is really our master; where is our home?"

What seems missed in all this is that Paul is writing to his Roman audience from a very different context than the contemporary question of whether or not to engage in politics. The Roman Christians were political, whether they liked it or not. The difference is that their politics of the church is witness, not control. The context is one of competing, not complementary, lordships. As was mentioned previously, Paul is writing to a people who have no power in government and are under an emperor who cares little for Christians. Nero was no friend to anyone who would dare upset the balance of power controlled by the Caesar. Though he was likely a young emperor at the time of Paul's writing, Paul does not seem moved to change his opinion when Nero later begins killing Christians for sport. The answer as to why Paul did not expend much ink on the rise of martyrdom in Rome in his letter to the Romans or any of his other later letters is found precisely in the text of his epistle to the Romans. The insight to understanding Paul's advice to the Romans in chapter 13 regarding government is found in his advice in chapter 12 regarding those who would oppose Christianity. In other words, Paul's advice to the Roman Christian martyrs is not to co-opt the power of governing authorities. His advice is to do good and die. Let us begin with a brief examination of Paul's description of the context of the Roman Christians' thought process.

The chapter break here has obscured a more appropriate reading of Paul's intentions. Romans 12 begins the flow of thought as follows:

> [1] Therefore I urge you, brethren, by the mercies of God, to present your bodies a living and holy sacrifice, acceptable to God, which is your spiritual service of worship. [2] And do not be conformed to this world, but be transformed by the renewing of your mind, so that you may prove what the will of God is, that which is good and

---

12. Ronald J. Sider and Diane Knippers, eds., *Toward an Evangelical Public Policy: Political Strategies for the Health of the Nation* (Grand Rapids: Baker, 2005) 363.

acceptable and perfect. ³ For through the grace given to me I say to everyone among you not to think more highly of himself than he ought to think; but to think so as to have sound judgment, as God has allotted to each a measure of faith. ⁴ For just as we have many members in one body and all the members do not have the same function, ⁵ so we, who are many, are one body in Christ, and individually members one of another. ⁶ Since we have gifts that differ according to the grace given to us, each of us is to exercise them accordingly: if prophecy, according to the proportion of his faith; ⁷ if service, in his serving; or he who teaches, in his teaching; ⁸ or he who exhorts, in his exhortation; he who gives, with liberality; he who leads, with diligence; he who shows mercy, with cheerfulness. ⁹ Let love be without hypocrisy. Abhor what is evil; cling to what is good. ¹⁰ Be devoted to one another in brotherly love; give preference to one another in honor; ¹¹ not lagging behind in diligence, fervent in spirit, serving the Lord; ¹² rejoicing in hope, persevering in tribulation, devoted to prayer, ¹³ contributing to the needs of the saints, practicing hospitality. ¹⁴ Bless those who persecute you; / bless and do not curse. ¹⁵ Rejoice with those who rejoice, and weep with those who weep. ¹⁶ Be of the same mind toward one another; do not be haughty in mind, but associate with the lowly. Do not be wise in your own estimation. ¹⁷ Never pay back evil for evil to anyone. Respect what is right in the sight of all men. ¹⁸ If possible, so far as it depends on you, be at peace with all men. ¹⁹ Never take your own revenge, beloved, but leave room for the wrath of God, for it is written, "VENGEANCE IS MINE, I WILL REPAY," says the Lord. ²⁰ "BUT IF YOUR ENEMY IS HUNGRY, FEED HIM, AND IF HE IS THIRSTY, GIVE HIM A DRINK; FOR IN SO DOING YOU WILL HEAP BURNING COALS ON HIS HEAD." ²¹ Do not be overcome by evil, but overcome evil with good.

In the midst of instructing the Romans toward the end of chapter 12, Paul suddenly begins to discuss the possibility of encountering hostile opposition to the loving lifestyle of the Christian. He has already called on them to "love without hypocrisy" and to "abhor what is evil" (v. 9). He continues by advocating love and a hospitality that builds an environment of gracious concern for other believers (vv. 10–13). He even extends a measure of grace to those who would be a source of persecution, calling on the Roman Christians to "Bless those who persecute you" (v. 14). This seems to be a turn from the internal to the external. Paul seems to be moving in his instructions from the internal activities of believers toward, and with one another, to the external activities of how the believers relate to those outside the church. This is confirmed later when he commands, "Never pay back evil for evil to anyone. Respect what is right in the sight of *all men*" (v. 17, emphasis mine). Paul seems to be moving progressively from the more comfortable environ of interaction amongst believers, though this is by no means easy, to the more hostile context of interacting with those outside the church. Paul recommends peaceful existence as a reflection of Godly virtues, even when others do not wish for peace: "If possible, so far as it depends on you, be at peace with all men. Never take your own revenge . . ." (vv. 18–19a).

Paul is laying out for the Romans more than simply a means to harmonious interpersonal relationships, though these are certainly good things. His remarks are aimed at a much higher goal. Paul wishes for the Roman Christians to build and maintain a solid trust in the sovereignty of God. When faced with strong opposition, Paul wants believers in Jesus to respond with an even stronger faith in the Lord's care and timing. Even in the face of being severely wronged, Paul leaves no room for taking matters into our own hands in a way that might seek a human notion of justice. Instead, he calls on believers to have restraint and patience as they wait upon the Lord to answer the wrong. "[L]eave room for the wrath of God, for it is written, 'Vengeance is mine, I will repay,' says the Lord." (v. 19b).

Paul is realistic about the probability of persecution. He expects the Roman Christians to encounter such strong opposition that they may be inclined to hate or dismiss their persecutors as beyond the possibility of being shown the grace of God. In the heat of the tension, Paul continues by calling on believers to show mercy to those who hate them, knowing that they too could come to repentance. However, even if they don't come to repentance, judgment belongs to God. The language Paul uses in the end of chapter 12 is a quote from Solomon in Prov 25:21–22, but the sentiment is reminiscent of the love of Jesus in the Sermon on the Mount, when He commanded His followers to "Love your enemies, and pray for those who persecute you, in order that you may be sons of your Father who is in heaven . . ." (Matt 5:44–45a). Paul's advice is simply stated, yet profound in its application. Though the Roman Christians may regard those in opposition as their enemies, the Lord calls on them to show mercy, ultimately a mercy that witnesses to the Lord of mercy. "But if your enemy is hungry, feed him, and if he is thirsty, give him a drink; for in so doing you will heap burning coals upon his head" (Rom 12:20). Paul does not continue the quote from Proverbs, but the sentiment may be implied, nonetheless. Proverbs 25:21–22 reads, "If your enemy is hungry, give him food to eat; and if he is thirsty, give him water to drink; for you will heap burning coals on his head, *and the Lord will reward you*" (emphasis mine). Paul does not mention the fact that the Lord will reward such a testimony to His mercy, but it is quite certain the Roman believers would have known this and relied upon it as a justification for their actions as they contemplated and measured how not to "be overcome by evil, but overcome evil with good" (Rom 12:21). God sees; God knows; God will keep account. However, even if the Roman believers would not have known of the possible reward awaiting them, Paul's point is still clear: Mercy in the face of persecution is the response of one who believes in God's control and power.

A question seems naturally to arise as we attempt to understand the implications of Paul's turn from the interactions of believers to the believer's response to unbelieving opposition. From where might such opposition arise? In other words, who could Paul possibly have in mind as he exhorts the Romans to trust in the ever-watchful eye of their Lord? The answer seems quite obvious as Paul continues his instructions in Romans chapter 13.[13] These chapters may seem like isolated teachings gathered for the sake of comprehensiveness toward the end of his thoughts for the Romans.[14] Certainly, Paul's words may apply to different venues as the Roman believers, and twenty-first century believers, embrace submission to the sovereign control of God. In other words, Paul's instructions may apply, at various times, to interpersonal conflicts as much or more than conflicts with the government. However, a clear single line runs through all these venues as he expects them to live in such a way that their dependence on and submission to the Lord is evident. Living the Lordship of Jesus before believer and unbeliever alike is Paul's commission to the Romans. With this in mind, let us examine Romans 13 in its entirety:

> [1] Every person is to be in subjection to the governing authorities. For there is no authority except from God, and those which ex-

---

13. Cf. James D. G. Dunn, *Romans 9–16*, Word Biblical Commentary (Dallas: Word, 1988) 759.

14. Douglas J. Moo, *Romans*, NIV Application Commentary (Grand Rapids: Zondervan, 2000) 414–15. Moo correctly identifies that Paul has a tendency at times to use "rapid fire" approaches to moral instruction, which may appear to create little connection between verses. However, it would seem here that Paul is not so eclectic in his collection of commands.

ist are established by God. ² Therefore whoever resists authority has opposed the ordinance of God; and they who have opposed will receive condemnation upon themselves. ³ For rulers are not a cause of fear for good behavior, but for evil. Do you want to have no fear of authority? Do what is good and you will have praise from the same; ⁴ for it is a minister of God to you for good. But if you do what is evil, be afraid; for it does not bear the sword for nothing; for it is a minister of God, an avenger who brings wrath on the one who practices evil. ⁵ Therefore it is necessary to be in subjection, not only because of wrath, but also for conscience' sake. ⁶ For because of this you also pay taxes, for rulers are servants of God, devoting themselves to this very thing.

⁷ Render to all what is due them: tax to whom tax is due; custom to whom custom; fear to whom fear; honor to whom honor. ⁸ Owe nothing to anyone except to love one another; for he who loves his neighbor has fulfilled the law. ⁹ For this, "YOU SHALL NOT COMMIT ADULTERY, YOU SHALL NOT MURDER, YOU SHALL NOT STEAL, YOU SHALL NOT COVET," and if there is any other commandment, it is summed up in this saying, "YOU SHALL LOVE YOUR NEIGHBOR AS YOURSELF." ¹⁰ Love does no wrong to a neighbor; therefore love is the fulfillment of the law.

¹¹ Do this, knowing the time, that it is already the hour for you to awaken from sleep; for now salvation is nearer to us than when we believed. ¹² The night is almost gone, and the day is near. Therefore let us lay aside the deeds of darkness and put on the armor of light. ¹³ Let us behave properly as in the day, not in carousing and drunkenness, not in sexual promiscuity and sensuality, not in strife and jealousy. ¹⁴ But put on the Lord Jesus Christ, and make no provision for the flesh in regard to its lusts.

Paul's admonition to submit, or obey, has been widely debated over the centuries. One side of the conversation focuses on what to do when the government is performing its responsibilities in a manner consistent with righteousness. When this is the case, submission is relatively easy. However, another side to the conversation arises more frequently, since governments have no commitment to proclaiming the Lordship of Jesus through conversion that leads to holiness. The typical question is "What should I do when the government asks me to do something that violates the clear teaching of the Lord in Scripture?" The answer is obvious from the Scriptures themselves. Peter and John did not stop witnessing of the Lord simply because the Sanhedrin didn't like it (Acts 4:19-20; 5:29).

The Performance of a Lifetime

Likewise, Daniel's friends did not bow to Nebuchadnezzar's statue, even when faced with the threat of death (Daniel 3). Scripture is clear that it is always right to obey God, if faced with the option of obeying men and defying God. Certainly, the question of what to do when faced with opposition from the government arises because of confusion, but even more, it arises from fear of consequences. Paul's instructions do not contradict the Christian's responsibility to obey God first and foremost. "Submit" to governing authorities seems a better translation than "obey" here, since submission may take the form of willingly following their edicts or willingly embracing the consequences for not obeying.[15] To "submit" is broader and far more inclusive than to "obey." When faced with tyrannical or evil regimes that are opposed to the clearly stated will of God, we willingly embrace death, which is still submission to governing authorities. What must be remembered is that the whole of chapter 13 regarding relationship with the government must be read in light of the admonition in the end of chapter 12 to leave vengeance in the hands of the sovereign Lord of the universe. Paul's point is that our temporal and finite nature may not grasp the universal import of what God is doing.

Bringing this back to our contemporary context, the issue usually discussed in light of the relationship between chapters 12 and 13 of Romans is the issue of compatibility. Is it possible to be a Christian and be involved in the various governments that may rise and fall in any period of history? Obviously, it is possible, since Daniel was able to maintain advisory positions in various governments (Daniel chapters 2 and 6 detail his service to two different kings from two different kingdoms). On the other hand, Daniel was never committed to these governments in a way that tied his own destiny to that of the state. The lion's den illustrated his commitment to the God who is over all nations (Dan 6:16-28). Daniel's great message is that government employment is possible, unless it challenges or competes with our allegiance to the Lordship of Jesus. More to the point of our discussion, did the apostle Paul expect the Roman believers to have such compatibility with the Roman government? We have one clue in the passages of Rom 12 and 13 that seems to indicate Paul's expectations. In Rom 12:19, Paul prohibits the Roman Christians from pursuing revenge, which he claims is solely the right of God. In Romans 13:4, Paul recognizes that

---

15. Moo, *Romans*, 422, 429–30. Also see John Murray, *Epistle to the Romans*, The New International Commentary on the New Testament (Grand Rapids: Eerdmans, 1965) 148.

the state can use the sword as an instrument of God's vengeance. Such a contrast makes it evident that Paul would be unsympathetic to a believer who wielded the state's sword, claiming it to be God's vengeance. Paul excludes believers from such pursuits, though the sword is rightfully under the authority of the state. When I am asked about my feelings regarding the state's use of the sword, my response is "States will do what states are prone to do!" They will always act in their own best interests, since this is the nature of the state. Christians, conversely, are called to different commitments. Let me clarify this briefly.

Paul has called Christians not to seek vengeance (12:19—εκδικουντες), but he opens the door that the state may be used as an avenger by God (13:4—εκδικος). On the surface, this seems to allow for Christians to use the state or be used by the state to carry out vengeance. The difficulty with this position arises when we see that Paul's context in chapter 13 is Christians being subject to the state's use of the sword, not taking up the sword. Christians are to practice good so as not to fall under the sword of the state. This "good" Paul has already defined as not returning evil for evil. Only by living in such a submissive manner, even when the state exploits the Roman Christians' submission, can they hope to avoid the sword.

I am constantly asked the centuries-old question that is updated with every generation: "What would you do if faced with two evil options?" e.g., when asked by a Nazi SS agent to reveal the Jews hidden in your basement, etc. The dilemma rests on the assumption that one must choose between two evils, thereby sacrificing some measure of character. Of course, from our discussion thus far, we know a third option exists that maintains character and may result in a good. When faced with two evil options, my response is typically, "By the Lord's grace, I would die!" In the final analysis, preservation of life is not more important than preservation of character and testifying of the Lordship of Jesus before evil regimes. In this case, the witness may be silence, but we witness nonetheless by dying for the sake of honoring the Lord. I do not commend death for its rhetorical value (martyrdom carries no virtue in itself); I am simply attempting to give the biblical response when faced with a decision that presumes death is the greatest enemy – to be avoided at all costs. I am unwilling to grant the presumption that life is *always* better than death. Of course, the reason this seems like an outlandish answer is because we no longer have a community of believers who are formed by the reality of such a

The Performance of a Lifetime

costly faith, at least not in America. The church in America is shaped by its commitments to various rights and privileges, the loss of which creates a crisis of faith.

At first glance, Romans 13 reads as though Paul is making a promise to followers of Jesus that if they simply honor the wishes of governing authorities, all will go well for them. In a world with a righteous government, such as the one Jesus Himself will establish upon His return, a simple equation like this would be valid. Indeed, Paul does hope that all will go well for the Roman believers, if they submit to authority in a willing and humble manner. However, he also seems aware that the possibility for revenge against authorities may arise, or perhaps has already arisen (Rom 12:12, 17–21). As John MacArthur notes in his comments on these passages,

> Like the other conquered peoples, the Jews of Palestine were little more than Roman chattel, an underprivileged and oppressed minority. They had no voice at any level of government and little legal recourse for injustices. Consequently, many reactionary Jews were in constant rebellion against Rome, some outwardly and some only inwardly.[16]

When the compulsion to rebel arises, Paul says submit. Rebellion may take many forms. It may be due to sinfulness or wantonness for the "deeds of darkness" (13:12). However, rebellion may also be due to the desire for justice and self-preservation. Whatever the case, Paul says "Submit!" Submission may, likewise, take differing forms. It may come as embracing the rule of government. It may also take the form of embracing the consequences for an inability to obey. Both are a witness to God's care and both will result in testimony to His greatness. In the case of the Roman believers, the latter seems most likely.

In light of such a context, Paul advises, "Love does no wrong to a neighbor; therefore love is the fulfillment of the law" (13:10). It is interesting to note that fulfillment of the law seems to be held in higher esteem than the justice of the government. Paul appeals to the believers in Rome to keep the spirit of the law in regard to actions and attitude toward neighbor, rather than instructing them to rely on the government's system of meting out what is due. In other words, a fair implication seems to be that justice, i.e., fairness, is a minimalist approach to human politics in that it

---

16. MacArthur, *Romans 9–16*, 209–10.

only arbitrates based on what is due, or is perceived as due, another. Love goes above and beyond in that it seeks the other's best interest, ultimately testifying of a greater reality than present circumstance (13:11–14).

If a Christian were to read Romans 13 in the context of an emperor who despised and wished to kill Christians, one could see how Paul's argument seems directed at something higher than merely surviving in the midst of a government whose rule was not always "good" or representative of the God who established it. Paul does not expect the government to set the standard for the believer. Instead, he seems to be directing the Roman believers to a higher calling: witness to the God who is higher than government. Do not "resist authority" when called to account for belief in Jesus. Those who resist will be accountable to a higher authority than the government. Obviously, Paul would wish for the government to act in such a way as to seek the good of the One who established it, but such is not generally going to be the case. Likely, such was not the case for the Romans. The government was not made up of Roman believers; they could not presume righteous behavior from those in political authority. The government was not a Christian government, nor is Paul establishing an ideal here for eventually forming a Christian government. Democratic ideologies have caused us to read this passage as though Christians were somehow a part of the work God was doing through the Roman (American?) government. When we read this passage as though the government is a help to the church, we are forgetting that this same government to which Paul is asking the Romans to submit is the government that killed them (8:36) and imprisoned and finally killed him. For God's own purposes, He has established the Roman government to carry out its laws in a way that may seem harsh to the Roman Christians, but submission to the harshness is their calling. In other words, let us state it as baldly as possible: Nero was appointed by God to kill Christians. We should be familiar with such a notion, since Jesus Himself understood Pilate's authority in such a way (John 19:10-11). Pilate asked the silent Jesus, "Do You not know that I have authority to release You, and I have authority to crucify You?" Jesus responded by saying that Pilate's authority was from above. Then, He humbly submitted to Pilate's authority to have Him crucified. Jesus recognized that God had placed Pilate for such a time and work as this. The presupposition that makes this difficult for us is that we have come to believe that our lives are for a different purpose than Jesus's.

The Performance of a Lifetime

This is a slightly different perspective than the friendly face we typically put on Romans 13, but no way exists around this interpretation. Of course, what makes it sound harsh is our opposition to death and our expectation that God would prefer our witness to extend over years in a long life, rather than be cut short by martyrdom. In other words, as discussed above, we fear death more than God. These are presumptive notions born from the modern commitment to the value of the self, or perhaps they stem from a commitment to the primary virtue of evolution: mere survival.[17] Whatever the source for modernity, Paul does not seem to share such presumptions. Indeed, the early church did not seem to share such a commitment to survival. It is not until Augustine (354–430) that we have a reasoned defense of survival of the church and the state conjoined together from a Christian perspective.[18] Reading this passage as instructions to martyrs may be a good explanation as to how the early Christian martyrs were able to submit to their deaths with such calmness and a willing spirit. As seen above, they certainly viewed martyrdom as a perfecting of their faith. Perhaps many, in the same manner as Justin and Ignatius, viewed governing authorities as God's agents of that perfection. Even though Paul makes reference to specific circumstances, i.e., taxes, honor, etc., the circumstances do not dictate the attitude or the limits of submission. When the question arose as to whether or not it was right for Christians to be killed by governing officials, no room was left for debate. Submission may come at a high price, but Paul's teaching is clear and final here: submit to those in authority, even if they require the highest of costs.

Of course, the objection someone might offer at this point is to ask, "But doesn't the government serve to mete out God's justice? Isn't that the point of government as an instrument established by God on the earth?" Or more to the point of this study, "Isn't the American government God's instrument of justice, making it imperative that Christians contribute to its mission?" Aside from the blind presumption regarding the justness

---

17. It is beyond the confines of this study, but an interesting case could be made that modern science, specifically evolution, has powerfully shaped the commitment of the modern self to life as an end in itself, rather than a means to some greater end. The ultimate goal of survival of the biological self, when coupled with the primacy of the political self in Enlightenment anthropology and metaphysics, seems insurmountable, even for God. In such a context, martyrdom is not merely foreign; it is ludicrous.

18. Note here that Augustine is writing almost one hundred years after the Constantinian conversion of the church.

of government in such questions, my response is to ask of the nature of justice. In other words, what would we expect of a government when it comes to justice? Typically the Western government is called on to arbitrate or reward/punish. Both options are premised on the fundamental notion of fairness. Certainly, biblical justice may include fairness, and the Bible often uses such a notion of justice in the context of the poor and oppressed (e.g., Prov 11:1; 16:11). However, the archetypical model of justice for Christians is the cross. Justice is defined at the cross by what can be given, not what is deserved. Sacrifice, not rights or fair treatment, defines it. Perhaps a better definition of justice that brings honor to God's reputation is:

> Justice is the treatment of another according to the righteous character of God, which may mean calling to account or may mean taking the burden of the other's plight upon oneself, or both—not fairness or impartiality, which require a distancing from one another or a "blindness" to one another. Justice according to the cross requires a nearness or taking notice and then acting on behalf of the other.[19]

Make no mistake; the demand for Western justice is but a plea for our own demise. Those who wish to live in a society in which justice is the prime virtue will not finally be able to stand before the judge. Our plea before God should be for mercy, for only in mercy can we hope to avoid the long stare of justice over our own misdeeds. Shakespeare seems to have hit on this notion in his *The Merchant of Venice*. Warning Shylock against his demand for justice, Portia extols the virtues of mercy over the right to what we believe we deserve.

> The quality of mercy is not strain'd,
> It droppeth as the gentle rain from heaven
> Upon the place beneath: it is twice blest;
> It blesseth him that gives and him that takes:
> 'Tis mightiest in the mightiest: it becomes
> The thronéd monarch better than his crown;
> His cepter shows the force of temporal power,
> The attribute to awe and majesty,
> Wherein doth sit the dread and fear of kings;

---

19. I am here intentionally denying the blindness often associated with justice. Justice must be understood with God as the almighty arbiter, not some notion of fairness or individual rights.

> But mercy is above this sceptred sway;
> It is enthroned in the hearts of kings,
> It is an attribute to God himself;
> And earthly power doth then show likest God's
> When mercy seasons justice. Therefore, Jew,
> Though justice be thy plea, consider this,
> That, in the course of justice, none of us
> Should see salvation: we do pray for mercy;
> And that same prayer doth teach us all to render
> The deeds of mercy. I have spoke thus much
> To mitigate the justice of thy plea;
> Which if thou follow, this strict court of Venice
> Must needs give sentence 'gainst the merchant there.[20]

Shakespeare, like anyone who has faced the terrifying knowledge of personal deficiency, saw the final end of the unwavering pursuit of justice. It can result in nothing but the recognition that none are capable of meeting the justice that is ultimately required for a good society. Only in the One who is just can we hope to discover what our souls crave, but even then His justice will be meted out through the lens of His cross. Jesus's politics of justice can only be viewed through the shaded glass of His mercy. To stare at its intense heat with no mediation leaves the seeing blind.

In summary, the Roman Christians are here being called by Paul to an obedience to the government that would afford them a reputation of being submissive citizens, even when persecuted or killed by that same government. We should not misread Paul in this. Paul is not anti-government; Christians are to be in subjection and pay taxes, giving honor to those who are in authority. This will grant Christians a reputation that is a platform for further witness to the God who grants all authority. As law abiding citizens, they will be seen as helpful contributors to the social network of society. But when government makes claims that are rightly God's, and Paul has every reason to expect the Roman government will, then witness may take another form. Witness to a government who ignores God's righteous reputation, which is to say all governments this side of the millennial kingdom, does not take the form of revolution—far from it. Instead, witness takes the form of patient mercy and love—returning good for evil, trusting that God will keep any accounts necessary. This is a trust in God to direct the affairs of a world that pales in comparison to

---

20. William Shakespeare, *The Merchant of Venice*, Act 4, Scene 1.

His kingdom and presence. It is a trust that is calm and peaceful when faced with certain persecution and death for the name of Christ. It is a faith that sees opportunity in loss, rather than feels the sting of unfairness. Commenting on the attitude Paul is recommending to the Romans here, Doug Moo rightly recognizes the purpose of living as witness.

> [W]hat is clear is that believers are to cultivate an attitude of love that puts the focus on the good of the other person and not on the defense of our own rights, dignity, or even, perhaps, our very lives. Lived out consistently, the Christian community can become a genuine counterculture that serves as a witness to a world increasingly caught up in the spiral of violence.
>
> Americans demand the right to carry guns and use them because other people are. Poverty-stricken nations spend billions of dollars on weapons so that they can keep up with their neighbors. Our children are taught to defend themselves, to "fight for their rights," and so on. Jesus suggests a better way. While it would be utopian to think we can transform society by our attitudes, what the church is ultimately called to do is to be a witness.[21]

As the author of Hebrews reminds his readers in Heb 10:32–39,

> But remember the former days, when, after being enlightened, you endured a great conflict of sufferings, partly by being made a public spectacle through reproaches and tribulations, and partly by becoming sharers with those who were so treated. For you showed sympathy to the prisoners and accepted joyfully the seizure of your property, knowing that you have for yourselves a better possession and a lasting one. Therefore, do not throw away your confidence, which has a great reward. For you have need of endurance, so that when you have done the will of God, you

---

21. Douglas J. Moo, *Romans*, NIV Application Commentary (Grand Rapids: Zondervan, 2000) 419. Though Moo seems to see the logic of the non-violent implications in his statement, he does not see the non-violent position as necessarily biblical. Presumptions about passages like Romans 12–13 seem to be directing his thought. While he is certainly correct that God ordains both church and government, seeing them as complementary seems problematic in Romans 13. Moo finally seems to have an idealistic government in mind when he reads Romans 13. "If the state is God's instrument to accomplish his purposes, among them the punishment of wrongdoers, how can Christians be wrong to participate in that service?" (418). Moo has principlized Paul's teaching, rather than dealing with it in its immediate context. Would Moo, or anyone who takes this passage along such a vein, really ask the Roman Christians who work for the government to kill other Roman Christians for not bowing to Ceaser, as Nero commanded the government to do?

may receive what was promised. FOR YET IN A VERY LITTLE WHILE, HE WHO IS COMING WILL COME, AND WILL NOT DELAY. BUT MY RIGHTEOUS ONE SHALL LIVE BY FAITH; AND IF HE SHRINKS BACK, MY SOUL HAS NO PLEASURE IN HIM. But we are not of those who shrink back to destruction, but of those who have faith to the preserving of the soul.

Why should a Christian be willing to endure such hardship, and perhaps even death? The author of Hebrews here explains that something greater awaits the believer in the future. He goes on to explain throughout chapter 11, the "Hall of Faith" chapter, that such faith is a testimony to the greatness of the object of our faith, even when such testimony demands torture, persecution, and death (11:35–38). To "shrink back" is to do more than simply lose a possible future reward; it is to deface the testimony of God's greatness. Those who are unwilling to embrace hardship, suffering, embarrassment, shame . . . (the list is unending) for the sake of witness to their faith in Christ are those who, though they may preserve their life or property, will lose the Lord's pleasure, and perhaps even their own soul. As Jesus made clear,

> For whoever wishes to save his life shall lose it; and whoever loses his life for my sake and the Gospel's shall save it. For what does it profit a man to gain the whole world, and forfeit his soul? For what shall a man give in exchange for his soul? For whoever is ashamed of Me and My words in this adulterous and sinful generation, the Son of Man will also be ashamed of him when He comes in the glory of His Father with the holy angels. (Mark 8:35–38)

The recurring theme of Scripture is the glory of God in His reputation and our opportunity to participate in His magnification of Himself. This is joy for eternity, as we watch it become reality and crescendo beyond what is even imaginable. Jesus rejoices in this with us, if we do not "shrink back."

DYING A THOUSAND DEATHS

An obvious dilemma arises as we observe our plight in America and our relationship to martyrdom. The simple fact is that martyrdom does not exist for us, in part, because we have religious freedom and in part, because the church has been tamed by the state. Perhaps one day, we will lose our freedoms to such an extent that our property may be seized. Further, a few of us may even endure jail time for sharing our faith or be killed as we unswervingly testify to Jesus's Lordship above all other gods. Such possibilities are real, but heroic. We cannot imagine they would ever become the norm, nor would we wish for such a thing. We are content to casually testify of our faith, and at the same time to fight and kill for our right to believe as we choose to believe and our right to live in a world in which it is safe to believe. American Christianity seems defiantly willing to protect itself from outsiders, whether governmental or otherwise. Loving our enemies and "not resist[ing] him who is evil" (Matt 5:39) seem to be teachings for another era. We have moved beyond giving our lives for the faith; rather, freedom has advanced us beyond it. American Christians may still die as martyrs today, but not for the sake of their faith. Indeed, they typically die for the "right" to have a faith that is safe. To call on Christians to live as the martyrs of the first century lived seems illegitimate, since such a pacifistic existence would invite abuses far removed from a testimony to our faith. American Christians are simply unwilling to give up their lives or their safety for what appears to be a meaningless death. Jesus's words of non-resistance seem foolish, when we could be using our safety and power to promote so much more. One might even go so far as to say that taking Jesus's words literally would make Christians into "doormats" who would become easy prey to the world. Our fear of such a position is but a testimony to our disbelief in the sovereignty of God. We do not finally believe He is able, or perhaps He is unwilling, to take care of us. We are dissatisfied with taking the same path as Jesus, who though

> He was oppressed and He was afflicted,
>   Yet He did not open His mouth;
>   Like a lamb that is led to slaughter,
>   And like a sheep that is silent before its shearers,
>   So He did not open His mouth. (Isa 53:7)

Jesus did not cry out for justice, because He relinquished what He deserved so that He might vanquish what we deserve. We often forget that though Jesus's purchase of redemption cost Him His very life, the price was much higher than death. Death was the final payment, but Jesus endured much more before He breathed His last breath.

> Therefore, since we have so great a cloud of witnesses surrounding us, let us also lay aside every encumbrance, and the sin which so easily entangles us, and let us run with endurance the race that is

The Performance of a Lifetime

set before us, fixing our eyes on Jesus, the author and perfecter of faith, who for the joy set before Him endured the cross, *despising the shame*, and has sat down at the right hand of God. For consider Him who has endured such hostility by sinners against Himself, so that you may not grow weary and lose heart. (Heb 12:1-3; emphasis mine)

Jesus bore the shame associated with dying a sinner's death without defending Himself. He embraced the mocking and humiliation with love and forgiveness. He suffered and died alone, despised by those closest to Him. With this as our example to imitate, no room exists for individual rights or freedoms. Our claims for what we believe we deserve, our pleas for justice, must always be measured against the path established for us by Him; a path where no thought of the self is welcomed.

What about suffering and death that may arise from those who do not know of our testimony? Could we not resist or kill those who would kill us for some reason other than testimony to Jesus? The notion that one could die a death that is not a martyr's death—like that of a victim of a random crime or the victim of a surprise attack – or experience suffering that is not due to one's faith—like a random rape or robbery—presumes an existence that is not witness. The difference between missionaries who are killed in such circumstances on the field and someone who is killed in a Western democracy under precisely the same circumstances is merely geographical distance. Such a random death in the West is seen as a tragedy, because it did not have to be. Random deaths on the mission field are seen as part of the job. The presumption that those "at home" should be safe from such things and that such a death or suffering should be regarded differently simply exposes the fact that we do not conceive of our existence "at home" as witness.

Every death is an opportunity for witness, even if it seems random. Perhaps the witness may not occur in the midst of the death, but it can occur in the generations after death. The author of Hebrews reminds us of this as he speaks of the testimony of Abel. "By [faith] the men of old gained approval . . . By faith Abel offered a better sacrifice than Cain, through which he obtained the testimony that he was righteous, God testifying about his gifts, and through faith, though he is dead, *he still speaks*" (Heb 11:2, 4, emphasis mine). God testifies of Abel's righteousness, because it is finally a testimony of His own righteousness (Matt 5:16). Abel died a senseless death; at least that is how it appears to us. When we read of how his brother killed him for making the better sacrifice, we think his death a waste, because we see no words or testimony during his death that may have given it a more identifiably Christian character, nor do we see that anyone else witnessed Abel dying for his faithfulness to God. All we see is that he was doing what God had asked of him. There was no flare or flash to his sacrifice. There were no crowds to observe his righteousness. He simply died before the Lord, doing what He had asked. Such a testimony is recognized only by God, since no human (except for Abel's killer) was present to record the exact nature of the events. God's declaration that Abel was righteous in his sacrifice and, ultimately, in his death, points the way for us today to consider how our lives might be regarded as righteous, even in the everyday habits of living. Life is worship; the praise is in the little things we do and say. Death, even the nonsensical death, can have meaning, if we live life before God in this way. He is our primary audience. The significance of God's observance of our lives and our deaths should not be underestimated.

When we talk of a death that doesn't "make sense" as a testimony, i.e., a random act of violence, doesn't that constitute a different sort of death? In other words, is it still martyrdom if only God and the killer see it and the story never gets out? What if no one is ever converted because of my death? Let's make this as hard as possible: "What if I'm killed in my home by a thief who has no idea I'm a believer? That's not preaching the Gospel! That's not really martyrdom, is it?" In answer to these questions, we must start by addressing the concern of witness. We know that the audience is much larger, since angelic beings witness our faith and faithfulness on earth (1 Cor 4:9; Eph 3:10). Witness may not always be for the sake of salvation. The testimony we provide is observed by God and the angels. It is a testimony of faithfulness for the believer to "take up his cross daily" (Luke 9:23). Certainly the killer(s) would also witness our death, and this may be significant. However, we cannot slip into a purely utilitarian argument where martyrdom is only meaningful if someone is saved as a result of it. God is glorified in even the most random of deaths when His saints are following after Him at the point of death. We can have no greater audience than God Himself. In the final analysis, our deaths are most meaningful in light of His understanding of them. From His perspective, death is never random and witness is never ceasing. He calls us to be faithful to walk in His way, whether we face violent persecution in the jungles or random acts of violence in the streets where we live. Our testimony and willingness to "take up *our* cross daily" is real in both scenarios. No death is a waste or meaningless when gauged from God's perspective. The question is one of faithfulness, or truthfulness, not one of circumstance. If we die serving the Lord, our witness is true, our martyrdom is real, even if no human who watches our death sees it that way. Death cannot silence a testimony to the heavens of a life well lived. Perhaps this focuses the question a bit better for us: How are we living? Do we see every day as a life of witness, or do we consider certain parts of our life as a "time out," a "day off" from living for the Lord?

From our perspective, we tend to see death as an end to witness; when in fact, it may be just the beginning. Death may be an invitation to witness for people with whom we never before would have had contact. The reason we miss this is because we isolate death as an event. Certainly, death is an event, but it is more than that. It is a testimony to life. Our death is *always* a statement about how we lived. The legacy of a eulogy is a testimony to death as a fulfillment of life, even for those who may find death prematurely. Death can open doors of witness life never will. Those who can accept this, who can "take up *their* cross daily," know that death is not the final enemy. Instead, our final enemy is God, if we have not discovered that His glory and His reputation are far superior to any life lived in this world (Matt 10:28). Our joy, indeed our calling, is to discover this while we yet have days to live and direct our lives in such a way as to draw attention away from the self unto Him.

I wonder if our aversion to such thinking (i.e., martyrdom, non-resistance, etc.) is grounded in the presumption that we are called to "maintain" or "preserve" the peace. We perpetuate the myth that all is well (cf. Jer 6:14; 8:11). The biblical truth is that we do not have peace and never will have it this side of Christ's return. We have a real enemy (1 Pet 5:8). We are in a real war, though we don't use bullets and bombs (Eph 6:12ff.). We suffer casualties and become wounded. When this occurs, we need very real healing, sometimes even physical healing. Many bear the scars of this war physically, mentally, and emotionally. The "peace myth" tends to blind us to the reality of the war in our midst every day.

CONCLUSION

The power of death is overwhelming. It can silence the loudest scoffers and pain the strongest heart. It's finality conquers the dreams of the most ardent optimist. In the face of such deafening strength, nothing is heard beyond the emptiness left in each of us. But a voice still speaks in death. It is the voice of hope and comfort. It is the voice of peace and trust. The Lord's voice, though many ignore it, is never drowned out by death. This kind of power is not politically motivated to "prop up" some temporal regime or political ideology for the sake of the longevity of the state. Indeed, the irony of dying for the sake of an ideology of self is that it leaves the future void of, at least, one life; it is no longer ideal for the one who is dead. Though we console ourselves in the thought of sacrifice for the sake of others, the greater good cannot replace the loss. However, in the politics of eternal Lordship, death is a means to an end well beyond the temporal. It is a testimony to the greatness of God, whether it be a death unto eternal life in heaven with Him or a death unto judgment. Obviously, one is preferable to the other. The point is simply this: Life and death are but moments of testimony to God's supremacy, His Kingship. In political terms, this is ultimate power and control. However, to state it so starkly misses the point of His purposes in maintaining such power. God's power to reconcile is not power for power's sake. Its goal is always worship. The final telos, or goal, of the universe is worship. It is for the sake of His glory that we are given life and that life is transformed into a new life at death. Praise of His name is the crescendo of all that exists in the universe. Some voices may be louder, some softer, some lives may be clearer testimony, others more remote, but all things material and immaterial can and shall worship the Lord and Sovereign of all creation. Politics, as we know it in America, ends where worship begins, because the power of worship is beyond the human. In fact, worshipful existence is, in a way, the anti-politics of America in that it ascribes power rather than proclaims it. Worship is self-abasing and humbling. At the same time, it is the most powerful and political act we can perform, because the Lord is King!

Subject Index

Abortion, 4
Alliance Defense Fund, 4
Amish, 119
Anarchy, 9
Anthropocentric, -ism, xvi, xvii,
　xviii, 26, 32, 33, 78, 88
Arab, 92, 95
Armageddon, 109
Asian, 95
Autonomy, -ous, xv, xvii, xviii, xix,
　2, 17, 20, 21, 22, 31, 32, 34, 37,
　43, 72, 74, 90, 99, 103, 104,
　111, 119, 120, 130

Baptize, -ism, 18, 29, 40, 41, 71, 82,
　83
Bill of Rights, 30

Caesar, 8, 13, 34, 121, 132
Capitalism, 74
Chiliast(s), 11,
Christendom, 2
Christian Coalition, 5
Christocentric, xviii, 120
Christology, 3, 55, 87
Citizen, -ship, 2, 8, 10, 14, 18, 91, 115,
　131, 143
Civil Rights, 16, 69
Common Good, 10, 37, 38, 72, 75,
　76, 89, 132
Communist, 4
Conscience, xii, xviii, 46, 67, 69, 70,
　71, 72, 73, 74, 75, 76, 81, 93,
　95, 136

Constantine, -inian, 2, 4, 11, 13, 14,
　15, 21, 22, 29, 34, 35, 36
Constitution, United States, xviii, 27,
　30, 31, 69, 70, 74
Conversion, xii, 2, 6, 25, 31, 37, 39,
　76, 124, 137, 141
Correspondence (theory of truth),
　49, 50, 63
Covenant, xiii, 5, 31, 77, 79

Declaration of Independence, 30,
　32, 74
Deconstruct, -ionism 21, 22, 24
Democracy xi, xiv, 14, 18, 19, 20, 22,
　32, 37, 68, 74, 124, 147
Democrat, -ic xvii, 2, 3, 18, 22, 30, 71,
　103, 140
Dispensational, -ism 5

Ecclesiology, 3, 5, 28, 37
Edict of Milan, 9, 36
Egalitarian, xvii, 23, 53, 70, 78
Eschatology, -ical, 3, 13, 17, 40, 50,
　52, 102

Fair, -ness, 5, 8, 9, 11, 25, 110, 111,
　140, 142, 144
Family Values, 23, 25, 28, 29, 76
Fear—Power, 92, 93
First Amendment, xviii, 69
Flag, 27, 32, 35, 38, 91
Focus on the Family, 4, 13, 14, 26
Foundationalist, -ism, xvii, 21, 61, 62
Fundamentalist, -ism, 3, 5, 13, 15,
　34, 42

Subject Index

Gnostic, -ism, 25, 46, 55, 64, 75, 76, 129
Gross National Product, 117–18
Guilt—Innocence, 92–94, 96

Hedonist, -ism, 98, 99, 103
Holy Spirit, 37, 38, 79, 100, 101
Homosexual, 4, 93

Idol, -atry, -ous, xiv, 7, 26, 28, 29, 61, 63, 65, 78, 80, 84, 98
Independent, -ce, 37, 62, 71, 110

Jerusalem, 5

Legal, 4, 48, 81, 82, 83, 92, 94, 113, 139
Liberal, xiv, xvii, 2, 4, 15, 23, 27, 28, 31, 33, 37, 38, 42, 51, 53, 54, 62, 65, 70, 75, 76, 87, 90, 130, 133

Manifest Destiny, 15,
Martyrdom, xvi, xviii, xix, 34, 35, 36, 114, 115, 119, 120, 121, 122, 123, 124, 125, 126, 127, 129, 130, 132, 138, 141, 146, 148, 149
Missionary, -ies, 17, 35, 73, 147
Moral Majority, 5

Nazi, 28, 54, 138
Nicea, 36
Non-foundationalist, 61

Objective, -ist, -ism, xvii, 31, 42, 44, 45, 46, 49, 50, 55, 56, 61, 64, 65, 105, 107

Pacifism, 42, 146
Patriot, -ic, -ism, 5, 17, 26, 38, 71
Persecute, -tion, 18, 67, 114, 115, 116, 121, 125, 126, 133, 134, 135, 143, 144, 145, 149

Pharisee, 4, 28
Pilgrim, 6, 15
Pledge, 4, 35, 38, 91
Pluralist, -ism, xvi, xviii, 22, 47, 48, 63, 65, 67, 68, 72, 75, 76
Post-millennial, xvii, 5, 10, 11, 15, 17, 35, 37
Pre-millennial, 4, 5, 14, 15, 16, 17, 20, 32
Privatize, -ation, xviii, xii, 71, 76, 89, 130
Proleptic, 87, 102
Proposition, -al, 50, 51
Providence, 1, 2, 17
Public Square, xvii, 24, 43, 44, 72, 76
Puritan, 15, 70, 74
Postmodern, -ism, xiv, 21, 22, 23, 48, 49, 66, 72

Reconcile, -iation, xviii, 5, 42, 109, 110, 150
Relative, -ism, 23, 29, 45, 49, 50, 60, 61, 62, 65, 72, 77, 92, 136
Republican, 1, 2
Revelation, xv, xvii, 22, 23, 24, 37, 43, 45, 50, 52, 53, 61, 62, 63, 65, 66, 70, 72, 79, 87, 125
Revolution, -ary, 11, 17, 34, 39, 41, 144
Rome, 8, 121, 126, 127, 128, 132, 139, 140
Roman Catholic, -ism, 5, 9, 11, 71,

Self-determined, -ation, xiv, xv, 32, 37, 90, 103, 130
Self-esteem, 95
Shame—Honor, 92–93
Sojourner, 6, 15, 39
Social Gospel, 29, 33, 38, 42, 43, 75, 132
Sovereignty, xvii, 8, 16, 17, 33, 36, 65, 103, 117, 119, 134, 146
Subjective, -ist, -ism, xvii, 45, 46, 48, 50, 60, 61, 62, 63

Subject Index

Theocracy, 18, 19
Traditional Values, 15, 23, 24, 25, 28, 29, 43, 76
Trinity, 12, 106, 107

Virginia Act for Establishing Religious Freedom, xviii, 71, 73

Westminster Confession, 97, 98

Name Index

Abel, 147, 148
Adams, Carole G., 23
Adams, John, 71
Allen, Barry, 48
Allen, Ronald B., 36
Aristotle, -elian, ix, 28, 38, 48, 50, 51, 98
Athanasius, 66
Augustine, 10, 141

Balmer, Randall, 18
Barth, Karl, 87
Beasley-Murray, George R., 40
Bryan, William Jennings, 15, 19
Bultmann, Rudolf, 23, 52, 53

Cain, 148
Calvin, John, 9, 71
Carey, Matthew, 73
Clinton, Bill, 19
Craig, William Lane, 49, 50, 52

Daniel, xvi, 16, 32, 35, 137
David, 36, 40, 81, 86, 88, 118
Descartes, René, ix, xv, 22, 44, 46, 61
Dobson, James, 4, 5, 14, 15, 16, 24, 25, 29, 30, 35
Domitian, 126
Douthat, Ross, 19
Dowse, Edward, 73
Driver, Tom F., 75
Dulles, Avery, 11
Dunn, James D. G., 135

Erickson, Millard, 15

Falwell, Jerry, 24
Forsythe, Clarke, 76
Freud, Sigmund, 33

Goldberg, Michelle, 18
Gore, Al, 2
Greenhow, Samuel, 73
Groothius, Douglas, 49, 54, 56, 58

Hagen, Kenneth, 12
Hauerwas, Stanley, ix, 12, 13, 16, 31
Heide, Gale, 88
Henry, Carl F. H., 3, 15, 25

Ignatius, 125, 126, 127, 128, 129, 141

Jefferson, Thomas, xviii, 3, 4, 30, 69, 70, 71, 72, 73
Justin, the Martyr, 121, 122, 129, 141

Kant, Immanuel, ix, 28, 29, 30, 31, 33, 48, 51, 65, 75, 98
Kennedy, James, 4
King, Martin Luther, Jr., 16
Knippers, Diane, 132

Lambert, Frank, 70, 73, 74
Lewis, C. S., 7, 52
Locke, John, 48, 70, 71
Luther, Martin, 10, 11, 12, 71

MacArthur, John, 25, 26, 27, 31, 33, 34, 116, 139
Madison, James, 30, 69, 70, 73

Name Index

Michaels, J. Ramsey, 40
Minnery, Tom, 13, 26, 29, 32, 34, 35, 36, 76
Moltmann, Jürgen, 87
Moo, Douglas, 135, 137, 144
Moore, Russell D., 3, 5, 25
Moreland, J. P., 44, 46, 49, 50
Morris, Leon, 40
Moses, 18, 56, 82, 104
Mott, Stephen Charles, 76
Muller, Roland, 81, 92, 93, 94, 95, 96, 97, 113
Münzer, Thomas, 11
Murray, John, 137

Nebuchadnezzar, 137
Nero, 8, 9, 10, 132, 140, 144
Nussbaum, Martha, 70

Oberman, Heiko A., 11

Pannenberg, Wolfhart, 87, 88, 102
Phillips, Kevin, 18
Pilate, 46, 47, 57, 63, 140, 141
Pinocchio, 63
Piper, John, xiv, xviii, 97, 98, 99, 102, 103, 106, 107, 113
Plato, 28, 64

Ponnuru, Ramesh, 4
Rahner, Karl, 107
Rauschenbusch, Walter, 75
Reich, Robert, 19
Roberts, Charles IV, 119
Robertson, Pat, 4, 5
Rudin, James, 18
Rush, Richard, 73
Rusticus, 121, 122, 123

Sanford, Charles, 73
Shakespeare, 83, 111, 112, 142, 143
Sider, Ronald J., 132
Smith, Mrs. Samuel Harrison, 73
Smith, R. Scott, 62
Steinmetz, David C., 11

Tenney, Merrill C., 40
Trajan, 126

Van Til, John, 70

Washington, George, 30
Williams, William, 70, 74
Winthrop, John, 74
Wittengenstein, Ludwig, 54, 59
Wolterstorff, Nicholas, 9, 10

Scripture Index

OLD TESTAMENT

Genesis
1–11	77
6:6–7	81
12:1–3	36
12:2	77
17:16	77
38	112

Exodus
20:2	80
20:3	80
20:5	80

Leviticus
11:44	77
19:2	77
20:7	77
26:13	96

Deuteronomy
15:6	77

1 Chronicles
21	36

2 Chronicles
7:14	17

Nehemiah
9:5	89

Job
13:15	125
38–41	101
38–40	103

Psalms
27:4	86
50:10–12	106
96	77
100:3	31
139:1–4	80
139:2–4	68
139:13–16	118

Proverbs
11:1, 16:11	142
21:1	103
25:21–22	134, 135

Ecclesiastes
7:25	55
8:9	55

Song of Solomon
2:1	84

Isaiah
9:6	42
9:6–7	39
26:8	77
40:12–17	105, 106
40:13	55
42:11	77

Scripture Index

Isaiah (cont.)

43:7	98
49:6	78
52:11	78
53:7	146

Jeremiah

1:5	118
6:14	149
8:11	149
16:1–2	117
16:3–4	117
31:31–34	79

Ezekiel

36:22–32	31
36:22–28	78
36:22–27	xiv, 105
36:27	31

Daniel

3	35, 137
4:17	16
4:25	16
4:34–35	16
6:16–28	137
7:14	16

Hosea

14:4–9	84

Joel

2:28–32	79

NEW TESTAMENT

Matthew

1:3	112
4:1–11	18
4:8–9	39
5:16	99, 107, 148
5:39	146
5:44–45a	134
5:48	60
6:28–33	85
7:15–16	64
10:24–33	9
10:28	117, 149
10:34ff.	27
10:34–39	28
12:46–50	27
16:24	123
16:26	128
18:1–6	29
18:15–20	30, 105
22:15–22	13, 34
25:31–46	108
26:36–46	18, 39
28:18	88, 102

Mark

3:14	63
8:34	123
8:35–38	145
10:13–16	29, 124
10:14	124
10:35–37	39
10:42–45	42
10:45	88, 120

Luke

2:8–14	80
4:14–21	40
9:23	123, 148
9:51–54	39
10:27	55
14:25–35	27
18:15–17	124
18:16	124

John

1:14	56
1:17	56, 59
1:18	60
1:19–34	41

Scripture Index

John (cont.)

2:3–5	40–42
4:23–24	59
5:31	60
8:1–11	105
8:31–32	56
8:40	57
8:44–45	57
8:41	80
8:44–45	58
10:17–18	82
12:27–28	101
14:6	57
14:9	60
14:16	100
15:18–19	115
15:18–21	xvi
16:7	100
16:13–14	57
16:14	88, 100
17:1–5	100
17:6–12	29
17:17	57
18:33–38	47
18:36	42
18:37b–38	57
18:38	63
19:10–11	140
19:26–27	29
19:30	82

Acts

1:6	39
2:16–21	79
4:19–20	137
5:29	137
17:24–25	106
17:25	108
23:11	8
25:11	8

Romans

1:16	83
3:23	96
3:24	96
5:8	107
6:3–5	123
6:3	83
6:15–23	xiii, 31
6:18	32
6:21	82
6:22	32
8:12–17	82
8:16–17	102, 107
9	111
9:21	104
9:22	111
12–13	141ff.
12	xix, 132, 138
12:4–5	104
12:5	103
13	xix, 8, 9, 10, 13, 14, 136, 139, 140, 141, 144
13:1–7	131
13:4	138
13:7	34, 35

1 Corinthians

1	62
1:18–31	66
1:27–29	53
2:14	53
4:5	80
4:9	148
5–6	104
7:8	28
7:25–35	28
11:1	38, 64, 104
12	104
12:12–31	103
15:54–57	82
15:58	83

2 Corinthians

4:18	127
5:18	42
6:17	78

Scripture Index

Galatians

3	77
5:22–23	100
6:9	83

Ephesians

1:4	101
2:10	88
3:10	148
3:21	89
5:11–13	80
5:25–27	105
6:12ff.	149

Philippians

1:10–11	87
1:21–23	131
2:1–16	31
2:4	103
2:5–11	xviii, 60
2:7	80
2:8	81
2:9–11	110
2:12–15	79
2:13	101
2:21–26	8
3:10–11	83, 123
3:20	14, 18

Colossians

1:13	82
1:16	80, 109
1:19–20	xviii, 109
2:15	82

1 Timothy

2:1–4	9, 13
2:1–2	7, 13, 114, 125
2:3–5	8
2:8ff.	8

2 Timothy

1:12	83
2:20–21	104
3:12	9, 114
4:6–8	8
4:7–8	114

2 Thessalonians

3:13	83

Hebrews

1:1–13	107
1:1–3	60
1:3–13	101
1:12	87
2:13	110
8:7–13	79
10:32–39	144
10:34	9
11:2	148
11:4	148
11:35–38	145
11:38	88
12:1–3	147
12:10	105

James

2:14	65
4:4	32

1 Peter

1:1	6, 39
1:12	100
2:6	96
2:11–12	6, 39
2:12	6
2:16	60
2:20–23	6
3:15–22	83
5:8	107

Scripture Index

2 Peter

1:4	86
3:9	78

1 John

1:6–7	58
1:8	58, 65
1:10	58
2:4	58
3:18–19	58

Revelation

2–3	104
12:10	80
19:7–8	104
19:11—20:15	109
20:7–15	108
21:24	39

www.ingramcontent.com/pod-product-compliance
Lightning Source LLC
Chambersburg PA
CBHW071457150426
43191CB00008B/1375